RENT *to* RENT

YOUR QUESTIONS ANSWERED

JACQUIE EDWARDS

Rent to Rent - Your Questions Answered

First published in 2015 by

Panoma Press Ltd
48 St Vincent Drive, St Albans, Herts, AL1 5SJ, UK
info@panomapress.com
www.panomapress.com

Book layout by Neil Coe.

Printed on acid-free paper from managed forests.

ISBN 978-1-909623-96-5

The right of Jacquie Edwards to be identified as the author of this work has been asserted in accordance with sections 77 and 78 of the Copyright Designs and Patents Act 1988.

A CIP catalogue record for this book is available from the British Library.

This book is available online and in bookstores.

DEDICATION & ACKNOWLEDGEMENTS

I want to dedicate this book first to my parents, Dan and Sue Edwards, who have always supported me. You always told me that I could do whatever I set out to do! Even when you thought I was crazy for quitting a well-paid and respected corporate job, you still stood behind me and believed in me. I would not have been able to achieve my current success without your constant confidence in me.

Also, I want to thank my wonderful partner, Anthony D'Souza, who has been beside me for this entire journey into Rent to Rent and property investing. His steadiness, analytical mind and wealth of business knowledge have helped keep me on track through all the ups and downs. It's been a great journey PoC and thanks for putting up with all the tears! I'm glad we were able to do this together and I couldn't have done it without your support.

And finally, thank you to everyone who submitted questions and helped me put this book together. It couldn't have been written without the help of our amazing coaching and mentoring clients and their encouragement. Helping you to build your property businesses and being able to share our learning with all of you keeps me focused and constantly growing.

FOREWORD BY SIMON ZUTSHI

I started to invest in property in 1995, doing it the hard way, on my own because there were no fantastic books like this, or courses or property network meetings where you can get support and help from other people. As a result it took me eight years to become financially independent by replacing the salary from my corporate job with passive income from my property portfolio. However, using the strategy outlined in this book, I have witnessed many people replace their income in as little as 12 months, including the author of this book, Jacquie Edwards, who has really mastered this particular strategy. I am delighted Jacquie has decided to share her experience and knowledge with you.

I meet thousands of new and experienced property investors each year, and without doubt the number one reason for most of those people wanting to invest in property is to replace their income so that they can spend their time doing whatever they want, instead of having to work for a living. This is closely followed by the number two reason for investing which is to build an alternative pension to give them financial security in the future.

In my opinion the very best strategy to achieve both of these outcomes is to invest in Houses of Multiple Occupation (HMO's) often know as Multi Lets. This is where, instead of renting out the whole property on one AST (assured shorthold tenancy) contract to a tenant, you rent out each of the individual bedrooms to a different tenant who is happy to live with other people and share facilities, such as the kitchen, a living room and the bathrooms. This strategy will generate far more income for you from each of your rental properties than traditional single let properties.

When done correctly, after all of the expenses, each HMO should generate anywhere between £500 to £1500 profit per month, depending on number of rooms, market rents and of course location. With this amount of profit per property, you do not need to have many properties to replace your income. For most people, having between four and six of these properties could be enough to replace their income. This is why HMOs are becoming such a popular investing strategy.

However, there are two problems with the HMO strategy. The first one is that it can be quite capital intensive to buy a property and get it set up in the correct way. The second issue is that it is more work and hassle than a single let property. This is the reason why the Rent to Rent strategy outlined in this book is so powerful. With this Rent to Rent strategy you don't need a huge amount of capital to get started and so it is a great way for you to discover if you like being an HMO landlord without having to make the large financial commitment of actually buying one.

The Rent to Rent strategy, when done correctly, can be one of the best strategies to quickly generate significant cash flow for you and that is how so many of my students have replaced their income in such a short amount of time. The one downside is that you don't actually own the properties, so it does not help you build a pension for the long term. Having said this, once you have gained some experience and track record using the Rent to Rent strategy it is often far easier to find and attract people who may want to joint venture with you or lend you the money to actually buy your own properties which can then be let out as traditional HMOs.

I often hear people say that certain strategies don't work in their area, and that may well be true for some strategies. However, with this particular Rent to Rent strategy, I know it will work in your area because I personally know investors who are successfully applying it all around the UK, including expensive areas like London, Edinburgh and Oxford where Jacquie has done so well.

Enjoy this book and take note of what Jacquie shares with you, as she really has become a master of this strategy.

Good luck on your property journey.

Best wishes,

Simon Zutshi

Author of *Property Magic*

Founder of property investors network

CONTENTS

SECTION 1: RENT TO RENT BASICS

7

SECTION 3: FINDING RENT TO RENT DEALS

SECTION 5: TENANTS

SECTION 6: EVERYTHING ELSE

HOW TO USE THIS BOOK

This book has been written as a guide that you can either read straight through or dip in and dip out of whenever you have a question. I've structured it in the order that you would be doing the process but you may need to skip forward or back depending on where you are in your property business and what you already know. The book is written in question and answer format and you can use the table of contents at the beginning to find the questions that apply to you.

I've answered the questions in as much detail as possible without making the book unmanageable and filled with legalese. Each Rent to Rent situation can be different and can be structured differently so it is impossible to cover all of the possibilities in a book. I've outlined some different options throughout the book and if you need more information feel free to book a FREE coaching call with me through my website www.JADESuccess.co.uk.

There is also a Resources section at the back with some useful pointers and recommendations of companies that I use and trust. Some of the links I provide may be affiliate links which means I might get some credits if you use their services, but wherever possible I've negotiated discounts for you when you use one of my links as well!

And a final note. This book explains the way I did things in my Rent to Rent business. I believe I have acted in the most ethical and responsible manner possible. There are other ways of running a business and other people may have different strategies. Rent to Rent is a new concept and laws and regulations are changing regularly. Property investing, like any business, can be risky. This book is for educational purposes only. The contents do not constitute financial or legal advice and you should seek independent advice when entering into any contract. This book is only a step in your education about Rent to Rent and property investing. See the Resources section for how to continue growing your knowledge and your business.

INTRODUCTION

Hello, I'm Jacquie. Thank you so much for taking the time to read my book (or at least pick it up and have a look). I am grateful for the opportunity to share my story and my learning with you and I sincerely hope that this book will inspire you and help you on your property journey!

Rent to Rent is a great strategy both for people who are just getting started in property investing and for people who already have experience and want an exponential boost to their cash flow. Rent to Rent is a very popular strategy right now and it's attracting more and more attention in the press. Lots of that attention is negative, based on the results of people who are uneducated and doing it incorrectly. Like any property investment strategy there are right ways and wrong ways of doing Rent to Rent, so well done to you for picking up this book to get educated and learn the right way!

I'll start with a little background on who I am and why you should listen to me.

Chapter 1: I was born... no, we won't go that far back. I'll skim through the first few years... I am from the US and I grew up in a small mid-western town where our main excitement in the evening was driving the "main drag", meaning basically we drove back and forth across town all evening. Not the most exciting and prestigious of beginnings.

I made my parents proud by getting good marks in school and deciding on a career as an accountant early on. Off I went to university at 18 and studied accountancy (in order to earn money) and literature (for fun). Following the path of a good worker brought up in the modern education system I was able to get a "good" job with PricewaterhouseCoopers (PwC), one of the largest accounting firms in the world. This was quite an achievement for a small town girl.

A few years gaining experience in the US and I was ready for a change of scenery. Luckily, I knew someone who knew someone in the London office and I got myself a two-year stint in England. Boy was that eye-opening. I arrived in London at the peak of the credit crunch. The work that my group did disappeared and things got a bit nasty in the office as people ran out of work to do and started getting competitive internally. Typical corporate atmosphere. So after being miserable and spending a lot of time either crying in the bathroom or drinking I decided to get out of there.

A few jobs in the accounting departments at some big companies and I realised I wasn't a very good employee. The thought of sitting forever at the same desk doing the same job for the rest of my life depressed me... A LOT! I got headhunted, switched companies and then left that company before my probation period ended. It was time to strike out on my own! *J. Edwards Accounting Ltd* was born. This was the next step up from being an employee – I was now a self-employed contractor. This meant I got to choose who I was working with, and when I wanted to stop working to go on an extended holiday it was much easier. My plan was to work for six months and travel for six months, rinse and repeat, living the dream!

This was great for the first few years. Getting contracts was easy for me in England because I was a specialist in US accounting so I was able to work with companies which needed to report to the US. I had a few jobs in the

London area and then I got the opportunity to work with a company in Oxford.

I didn't realise it at the time but my property journey really began while I was living in London (just before I headed off to Oxford). I did my first Rent to Rent on the flat I was living in. I did it incorrectly and broke lots of rules as I was uneducated and just didn't know any better. It started when my friend and I moved into a flat together. It had three bedrooms. When I was working it was just the two of us living in the flat (both of our names on the lease) and perfectly above board. When I wasn't working we got in another roommate − sub-letting the third bedroom. I suppose this is not too big a deal as lots of people do that. When my friend decided to move out I was then the only person on the lease and sub-let the other two rooms. Sometimes when I was travelling for a long period I even sub-let my bedroom! So basically I had an AST (assured shorthold tenancy) with the owner just for me and sub-let the bedrooms. A definite no-no since I didn't ask the owner for permission! But I didn't realise this was wrong at the time. And I definitely didn't make a profit as I still covered most of the rent and the bills (lack of education again). Completely the wrong way to do Rent to Rent in all aspects, but like many people who stumble into property, I didn't know any better and didn't realise that with a few tweaks I could do it properly and make a lot of money doing it!

Fast forward − I moved to Oxford for what was supposed to be a four-month contract. I kept the flat in London (sub-letting my bedroom) since I was planning to move back in a few months and I decided to find a house-share in Oxford. I fired up my laptop and got on Spareroom to message all the ads for "Professional" rooms that I could find.

I did my viewings and these rooms were DIRE! Most of them were terrible, dark and dirty. They were mainly old student houses which had non-students living in them. I was appalled. And the rooms were expensive too! Luckily, I finally found a nice place where the owner lived in the house so it was well looked after (although there was an incident of mushrooms growing in the shower... but a bit of bleach took care of that). It was that first view of the Oxford HMO market that stuck with me and was the catalyst for my property strategy a few years down the line.

As most consulting contracts do, my contract in Oxford was extended. And I realised I LOVED OXFORD! I am not a big city girl and didn't realise how much I didn't like living in London until I left. So I gave up my flat in London and settled in Oxford... well, after a quick three-month tour of West Africa on a big yellow bus, sleeping in a tent... I settled in Oxford.

Fast forward another two years and I was bored AGAIN at work. I was still in the same contract in Oxford which was supposed to last four months and was still going strong two years later. Everyone was great and it was nice enough as jobs go but I knew there must be something better out there. I dabbled a bit in setting up an accounting training company, but accounting is not the most exciting subject and I couldn't get into it!

My partner and I then educated ourselves in forex (foreign exchange) trading but quickly learned that it takes a lot of time and you really need to do it every day for YEARS before you can reliably make a profit. I didn't have that much time or capital to lose.

Then I discovered Simon Zutshi's book, *Property Magic*. Wow! It all sounded too good to be true. I had also read *Rich Dad Poor Dad* and knew he promoted property investing, so I figured if a couple of successful people say that property investing is the way forward then it must be true. This led me to my first PIN (property investors network) meeting. (If you want to go to a PIN meeting, check the Resources at the end of the book for more information and a code to attend your first meeting for free.) At my local Oxfordshire PIN meeting I met the host who is a ball of fire and energy! Her story inspired me, and after a few meetings I was ready to take the plunge into the three-day Mastermind Accelerator course. This did cost a couple of thousand pounds so it was a big step. I also dragged my partner along with me. He will admit that he didn't want to come at first, but he's happy I took him now!

Those three days blew my mind! There was so much information and such a great spirit of sharing I didn't know could exist in business. Coming from the corporate world where everything was so competitive and secretive and you pushed everyone out of the way to get to where you wanted to be, this whole sharing thing was quite new to me. And I LOVED IT! And luckily so did my partner. By the end of the three-day Mastermind Accelerator we were sold and signed up for the 12-month Mastermind course.

We were really lucky in that there were no places available on the course until six months later. So we were able to pay our fee (again a large investment) which enabled us to start our coaching right away. That extra six months of coaching was amazing and really helped us get results. I can honestly say that without my regular coaching calls I would never have accomplished what I was able to achieve... although it did take a while to start seeing results. We weren't overnight successes.

I had savings enough to live on for one year... so I had to make it work or I would be going back to accounting with my tail between my legs! We started our advertising right away; like everyone does after a great course, we were thrust into action by the excitement after the three days of training.

Then we took a three week holiday to Nepal...

And then over Christmas and New Year we spent three weeks in Australia...

And then... I came back in January and had my coaching call. I started by whining about how nothing was happening in my property business. It had been about six months, and apart from a couple of calls from nearly motivated sellers we had NOTHING! SIX MONTHS OF NOTHING! What my coach said next changed my life.

He asked, "When is your next holiday?"

My demeanour changed immediately to excitement (I love holidays) and I answered saying, "Well, in May we are planning.. blah blah blah..."

Then he asked, "And when are you getting your next house?"

And I started whining again, "I don't know." I told my coach, "I just can't seem to get any."

And here it is, the most eye-opening thing anyone has told me. He said, "Maybe if you planned your property business in the same way as you plan your holidays you'll get more out of it."

All the light bulbs started flashing. I was just waiting for a property deal to come in while I sat planning holidays. I figured my generic "We Buy Houses" advertising would bring me millions of leads in a rising market where everyone was jumping back into property and prices were increasing and no one was having trouble selling or renting their houses. I was researching every strategy under the sun because I thought I could do it all. I was also dabbling in network marketing because I thought that was amazing as well. Basically, every shiny penny someone put in front of me, I chased it! Lease Options, Purchasing, Instalment Contracts, Buy to Sell, Rent to Buy, Rent to Rent, network marketing, FX trading – I tried it all!

But it turns out that I wasn't actually doing anything! I was using my employee attitude of looking busy (while booking holidays and playing on Facebook) and not actually working on my business.

So Anthony, my partner, and I sat down and made a plan. We did some due diligence, and based on the results decided that we would do Rent to Rent in Oxford. For at least six months we wouldn't look anywhere else or at anything else. Then, after six months, if Oxford wasn't working, we could look into changing locations. We needed to replace my income quickly, and while we had some start-up capital, it wasn't enough to buy more than one HMO in the expensive Oxford market. This meant Rent to Rent was going to be our Year 1 cash flow strategy, and once we made a success of that we could move on to buying properties or doing flips or any other strategy.

I then got stuck in. We upped our marketing (I'll explain how to do that later) and the calls came pouring in. I was viewing 10+ properties a week and making offers on every one of them. Most of my offers were way too low and never had a chance of being accepted, but I made the offers anyway. Every time I talked to a property owner I was getting practice, and the practice made me better for the next time I talked to another property owner.

Slowly, very slowly, I built up the relationships with a few key property owners. It took months of relationship building before I got my first Rent to Rent agreement signed. But once you have that first one under your belt, the rest are SO much easier. Between April and August I signed eight Rent to Rent contracts. There are a lot of people who can do more, but I am awfully proud of that accomplishment because those HMOs are in an Article 4 area with additional licensing and in a town that rarely has rental voids. If I can do it in a tough market (and I'm no one special), you can do it in your market! Those eight Rent to Rent contracts also replaced my income and made it so I don't have to worry about going back to accounting! I am now financially free!

That's enough about me. This book is about what I learned over the past year about how to do Rent to Rent properly. There are quite a few folks who aren't doing it properly, and whether they are cowboys or just uneducated it doesn't really matter. I want to help lift the stigma from Rent to Rent by helping you to do it properly!

And remember – if you need some help, don't hesitate to call me. You can book a FREE chat with me through my website at www.JADESuccess.co.uk or book a longer call using the voucher code BOOK for a 20% discount!

SECTION 1:
RENT TO RENT BASICS

SUB-TOPIC 1.1: GETTING STARTED

Question 1.1.1: What is Rent to Rent?

I've been told the best place to start is at the beginning –
so we will start with the first question which is *What is Rent
to Rent?* Many of you may be beginners and have no idea
that you can replace your income using properties that you
don't own. Others of you will have a solid background
and knowledge of property investing from other books,
training courses, or your own real life experience. I'll
provide a brief outline here for those of you who might
be new to this strategy or new to property investing in
general.

In the simplest terms, people doing Rent to Rent are simply running a property management business. The Rent to Renter is managing the property for the property owner they *rent* the property from. Then the Rent to Renter puts their own tenants into the property, generally on a room by room basis. Rent to Rent is about controlling the asset rather than owning it.

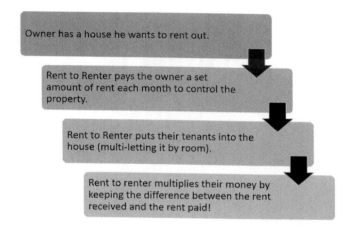

Owner has a house he wants to rent out.

Rent to Renter pays the owner a set amount of rent each month to control the property.

Rent to Renter puts their tenants into the house (multi-letting it by room).

Rent to renter multiplies their money by keeping the difference between the rent received and the rent paid!

Rent to Rent is a relatively new strategy in property investing. In my opinion, it is less of an investment strategy and more of a property *BUSINESS*. Rent to Rent is much touted as a "No Money Down" (NMD) or "Low Money Down" (LMD) strategy for property investors to use to get started when they don't have a lot of cash or capital behind them. I'm going to be pretty blunt and say that I completely disagree with it being a NMD strategy. You can get started using "Other People's Money" (OPM), which is true of any property investment strategy, but there will always be some costs involved, whether borne by the Rent to Renter or their investors. And one of the golden rules of property investing is to always make sure you have a cash buffer, so you should not jump into this strategy if you don't have a bit of cash to cover you in a pinch – whether this is your own money or OPM.

Question 1.1.2: Why would a property owner agree to do this?

I've found many people are limited by the belief that a property owner would never want to do Rent to Rent. Those people can't understand why a property owner would give you their property for a lower rental amount than they know is possible to get?

Let's stop thinking that way RIGHT NOW! There are many different reasons a property owner would want to do Rent to Rent. Here's just a few of them:

- They don't want the hassle of managing multiple tenants themselves

- They've been doing it themselves and can't manage multiple tenants and as a result are having a lot of stress and headaches

- They don't know that they can rent to multiple tenants for a higher rent

- They are attracted to a long-term commitment

- They want a passive income with no hassle

- They have voids and can't fill the house

- The house is in poor condition and they can't afford/ don't want to fix it up to attract the right tenants

RENT TO RENT - YOUR QUESTIONS ANSWERED

And those are just a few reasons. The key is finding the property owners who have a problem and helping to solve that problem with Rent to Rent. I'll explain more about how to find these owners in Section 3: Finding Rent to Rent Deals. Just remember, Rent to Rent isn't for every property owner – so you will get some "No's" along the way. You have to keep going to find the property owners who have a problem, and solve that problem!

Question 1.1.3: Isn't this sub-letting and isn't sub-letting illegal?

There are quite a few similar questions around the topic of sub-letting and the legality of Rent to Rent. Is Rent to Rent considered sub-letting or is it just property management? Also, who says that sub-letting is illegal? Is it the mortgage lender that doesn't allow sub-letting or is it the standard Assured Shorthold Tenancy Agreement (AST)?

First, let's understand what sub-letting is. Sub-letting is defined by the Citizens Advice Bureau (www.adviceguide. org.uk) as:

> Sub-letting happens when an existing tenant lets all or part of their home to someone else. That person is known as a subtenant, and they have a tenancy for all or part of the property which is let to them. They also have exclusive use of the accommodation that is let to them.
>
> When a property is sub-let, the owner is known as the head landlord. The tenant they rent to is called the 'mesne' tenant. Mesne means intermediate and is pronounced as 'mean'. The mesne tenant then rents to the subtenant.

So, sub-letting is quite simple in definition (if you ignore all the funny terms) – but is it legal? YES IT DEFINITELY IS LEGAL – if you do it correctly. There are no UK laws against sub-letting. The only things that would bar sub-letting would be:

- the type of contract between the property owner and the tenant

- the terms of the property owner's agreements with anyone else regarding the property (such as mortgage lenders).

Sub-letting vs. Property Management

If you have any kind of tenancy agreement with the owner (commercial lease, AST, etc.), then you are sub-letting (based on the definition we included at the beginning of this question).

If you use a management agreement, then you are simply a property manager and don't need to worry about sub-letting (like a letting agent).

Sub-letting and Contracts

So are you sub-letting or are you doing property management (like a letting agent)? If you check out Sub-topic 1.2: The Paperwork, we discuss contracts in a bit more detail, but basically I believe there are four main types of contract:

1. AST (Assured Shorthold Tenancy)

2. Commercial Lease

3. Management Agreement

4. Company Let Agreement

Depending on the type of contract you are using with the property owner, sub-letting can be in breach of your contract, so it is important to make sure you have the right type of contract in place.

You should create an appropriate contract for your situation. Generally, it is said that using a standard AST between the Rent to Renter and the owner of the house is not appropriate. It does depend how this is written. The following chart is based on information from www. adviceguide.org.uk and discusses when tenants are allowed to sub-let their rented homes.

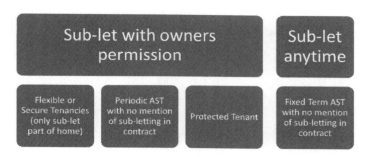

Technically, you can use any one of the above types of contracts for Rent to Rent as long as the contract doesn't say that you can't sub-let, but the contract will need to be reviewed to ensure that any clauses about sub-letting are not breached. See more about contracts in Sub-topic 1.2: The Paperwork.

Sub-letting and Mortgages

Meeting the terms of the mortgage is the property owner's responsibility. They will be the ones who know what type of mortgage they have (residential, buy-to-let, commercial, HMO, etc.). It is generally good to recommend that they make sure any agreement you would come to will not violate the terms of their mortgage, but you may not know exactly what their mortgage says. Also, you are not likely to be a mortgage or financial advisor to be able to provide them advice in this topic. If the owner is concerned, recommend that they speak to their mortgage lender or their mortgage broker as those professionals will be much better positioned to give advice on this topic. Be very careful not to provide financial advice as this is a highly regulated area!

I recommend that you make sure that the property owner has, as a minimum, a buy-to-let mortgage or a residential mortgage with consent to let. In some areas or with bigger HMOs the property will need to be licensed by the council, so it's best to make sure ahead of time that the lender will allow the property to operate as an HMO under the terms of the mortgage (councils can and do contact mortgage companies to ensure it is ok). (More details in the next Sub-topic.)

Sub-letting and insurance

I think the insurance is one of the most important things to consider in this situation. While the owner is ultimately responsible for making sure their property is properly insured, you will have a duty of care to your tenants. If the owner's insurance is not correct, is invalidated by your contract or invalidated by the number of people in the house, then you could be in trouble if something unfortunate happens and the tenants turn to you to make good after the insurance won't pay. Again, if you aren't a financial advisor or an insurance broker, you can't give the owner advice on insurance, so it would be good to make sure to have a clause in your contract that specifies what type of insurance they need and that it is their responsibility as the property owner to have the general building and landlord liability insurance that is suitable for multi-letting. If possible, get a copy of their policy to make sure none of your dealings are in breach of the insurance. Ideally, you can even be included as a named party on the insurance.

Bottom line – be open with the owner, and make sure they understand their responsibility with the mortgage and insurance and that the contract is appropriate for the specific situation you are in.

Question 1.1.4: How do I ensure the property owner pays their mortgage?

This ultimately comes down to an issue of trust. The first thing I would say is, never go into business with someone whom you don't trust. You are getting into a long-term relationship with this property owner. You will be bound together by a legal contract for a number of years. Make sure you first build a relationship and trust that person.

What if you don't meet them (i.e. you get the property through an agent) or don't have time to build a solid relationship? In this case you'll have to rely on your legal contract and the legal system. Also, make sure you ask the agent what due diligence they have done to make sure the owner is paying their mortgage and meeting their legal requirements.

But the agent's word isn't something you want to rely on. So I would recommend forming a good relationship with the owner. Or at least Googling them and making sure they don't have any horrible articles or dodgy details lurking online. I once had a potential Rent to Rent deal and didn't get the warmest fuzzy feeling from the property owner when I met him. When I went back and did my Google research I found quite a few news articles about his fines for basically being a slum landlord. I know there are landlords who make mistakes and don't know exactly what they are doing, so one or two fines might be forgivable. But there was a long trail of bad press about this guy. So I have crossed him off my list.

You can also set up different scenarios with the owner such as a joint bank account that you pay your rent into and he pays the mortgage out of, so that you can see the mortgage getting paid. Or you can ask for regular statements from the mortgage lender, etc. Depending on how complex you want to make it there are other ways of checking. But I would recommend understanding why you want to put any of these measures in place, and if it's because you don't have the warm fuzzy trusting feeling about the property owner, then maybe you shouldn't be doing business with them.

This trust issue comes up again when we talk about who takes care of the maintenance, so I recommend always building up a trusting relationship as you are in it together for the long haul. Don't do business with someone you don't trust. Accidents may happen and the owner may not be able to pay their mortgage one day, but if you have the relationship, hopefully they will let you know and you can help them (maybe with a BMV purchase or a lease option... but those topics aren't for this book).

SUB-TOPIC 1.2: THE PAPERWORK

Question 1.2.1: What contracts should I use with the property owner and what mortgage and insurance implications do they have?

Great question and good that you care about making sure the contract is right for the owner as well as yourself. There are quite a few things to think about, but at the top of the list I would say, "Keep it simple".

Let me elaborate a bit more on the different types of contracts you can have between yourself and the property owner:

1. AST (Assured Shorthold Tenancy) – not recommended for Rent to Rent unless it has been specifically tailored for you by a solicitor who has experience with Rent to Rent. An AST is the type of agreement that you would have with your tenants, not with the owner.

2. Commercial Lease – this is great when the property owner doesn't have a mortgage as many mortgages don't allow long-term leases. Again, this should be drafted by a knowledgeable solicitor and can be written to contain whatever clauses and terms you and the property owner agree on.

3. Management Agreement – this is the type of agreement letting agents will have with their landlord clients. This is more suitable when the owner has a mortgage as it is more commonplace and mortgage companies are used to management agreements. I still recommend that you have a good solicitor

draft your agreement. Please note that if you use this type of agreement, the income that you receive is management income and not rental income. Therefore it can attract VAT. Please make sure you talk to a good accountant.

4. Company Let Agreement – this is another type of contract that is generally not suitable for Rent to Rent. A Company Let is when a company rents a house from the owner for use by THEIR employees. Since you won't be putting your employees in the house you shouldn't use this type of agreement.

I use a mix of management agreements and commercial leases. I prefer commercial leases as the income generally doesn't attract VAT for us, but I tailor my agreements to the property owner's situation as much as possible.

Ultimately, it's up to the owner to make sure their mortgage and their insurance are suitable. In all my contracts I make it clear that it is the owner's responsibility to maintain the property's building and landlord insurance along with telling them to ensure their mortgage product is correct.

Now let's talk quickly about mortgages just so that you know a bit of the basics. Again, I'm not a mortgage broker and every mortgage has its own terms and conditions so every situation is different, but, in general, I like to think of three basic types of mortgage:

1. Residential Mortgage. This is the type of mortgage the house is likely to have if it is currently owner occupied. You will always want to make sure that the owner gets consent to let. This might not be something to delve into during your first conversation as a lot of people won't understand and this could scare them

away with complexity. But once you've come close to an agreement you will want to make sure that they speak to their mortgage company or that they give you permission to speak with the mortgage company to get consent to let. This may result in increased interest charges from the mortgage holder (which the property owner would need to pay) so make sure you get this sorted before you finalise any contracts.

2. Buy-to-Let Mortgage. This is the type of mortgage the property owner SHOULD have if the property is currently being rented out and the owner does not live in the property. It's good to check as accidental landlords may not know that they need a buy-to-let mortgage or consent to let. If you will be renting the house to a family, a single occupant, or an unlicensed HMO, this type of mortgage is generally fine.

3. HMO Mortgage/Commercial Mortgage. It's probably a lot more complex than this but I group these together as the type of mortgage necessary for a licensable HMO. It may also be necessary in a non-licensable HMO if you are renting each room on individual ASTs (Assured Shorthold Tenancy Agreements) or if there are locks on each door (different lenders have different criteria). If the owner has this type of mortgage, you are probably in the clear to rent it out as an individual room by room HMO, and as such this is probably the best type of mortgage for the owner to have.

Now that is a very over-simplified summary of mortgages. There are many more terms about contract lengths and types of tenants that I can't cover because there are so many different types and I don't have enough space in this book. And, unless you are a mortgage broker, you can't give advice to the home owner about their mortgage so you probably don't need much more information than this. You could ask the property owner (once you have built up enough rapport) if you can have a read through of their documents, but I suggest that it is enough to understand which of the basic types of mortgage they have and make sure they have consent to let at the very minimum. If you need an HMO licence for the property, you will need to make sure the property owner's mortgage company is ok with that because as part of the HMO application process many councils will contact the mortgage lender.

I think insurance is a much more important topic. While the mortgage is important, generally as long as the mortgage company is getting paid the lender won't cause a fuss. And if you or the owner have spoken with the mortgage company and have their permission, you should be all set. So let's move on to insurance, again with a disclaimer that I am not a financial advisor or a qualified insurance person, so I recommend you speak with someone in the insurance business who can help you with your exact insurance needs.

Insurance is important for the safety of all parties in the contract. For the safety of the owner and his asset, for yourself and for your tenants. You need to make sure all of you have the correct insurance products in place. In fact, it's so important that I think you need to make sure you have an insurance expert on your power team as there are so many options and it depends what you are doing with the house and what your specific situation is. I don't think this is something you need to discuss with the property owner at the first meeting, and it can probably wait until after you've signed contracts. But make sure your contract has a clause that stipulates that the owner must properly insure the house with building and landlord liability insurance. And then, depending on the type of contract you are using and how you run your business (sole trader, limited company, etc.), make sure you speak to an insurance broker about what type of insurance you need! Normally public liability is a must and possibly also professional indemnity.

Question 1.2.2: How can I create a contract that would let me out quickly if I am not able to find tenants?

Any kind of contract should be able to give you a get out clause – you just need to draft it correctly. Your solicitor could help you draft a break clause properly. I just add a simple clause that says that I (as the tenant or the managing agent) may terminate the agreement with the earliest termination to be twelve months after the start date by giving at least six months previous notice in writing to the Property Owner.

You can give yourself one month, two months, or twelve months if you like – whatever you agree with the owner and feel comfortable with yourself.

Hopefully, you will never need this clause because you have done all of your research and you fully understand your market (see Section 2: Choosing Your Area). But it never hurts to add a break clause on your side just in case things go wrong or you just get tired of it – who knows what could happen a few years down the line.

As a side note – I don't offer a standard break clause for my property owners. They are tied in for the full term of the contract. Some owners have asked for a break clause and I have told them I could provide it, but it would attract penalties. I generally say something like: "Because we spend quite a bit of money upfront refurbishing your property, we don't make a profit in the first year. We are happy to offer you a break clause, but we would need to add a penalty attached to it to ensure we don't lose money." This reminds them that you are a business and that you will be increasing the value of their home. We've toyed with break clause penalties of a multiple of whatever the current rent is at the time. So, for instance, if they wanted to break the contract at month 18 then they would need to pay six times the monthly rent. But if they wanted to break the contract in month 55 then it would only be two times the monthly rent. And no matter what, you should always make them give you at least six months' notice so that you can give your tenants the legally required notice to vacate (six months is the minimum legally enforceable term of an assured shorthold tenancy agreement).

Question 1.2.3: What kind of insurance do the property owner and I need?

I've included insurance in some of the previous questions, and I think insurance is one of the most important things to be clear about in your dealings with the owner.

Building and Landlord Liability Cover:

While this type of insurance is ultimately the responsibility of the property owner as they are still the owners of the house, you also have a duty of care to your tenants. You can be named in the policy as an interested party, which could be useful down the road, so discuss that with the owner and insurer if you'd like more involvement.

You also need to make sure (or have the owner make sure) that renting the house as an HMO does not invalidate the insurance. If the house is currently used as the owner's family home, they will likely only have a home owner's insurance policy. You will need to change this to a landlord policy which will cover public liability in case of any injuries to tenants and guests. If the house is currently rented as a single let, you will need to ensure that the insurance will cover multiple tenants on separate ASTs.

Next, you need to make sure any contract that you have with the owner does not invalidate the insurance. If you are using a management agreement, this is likely much easier as it's quite common. If you are using any sort of tenancy agreement (commercial or AST), it becomes a bit more important to make sure the insurance company is clear on what is happening and that they will cover any issues that might arise.

Insurance that you (the Rent to Renter) need:

Again, this will depend on your circumstances and is quite a general requirement.

With regard to the specific property, the owner is responsible for the insurance, but as I mentioned above you can be a named party on the policy. You may also agree to pay for all or a part of the insurance, in which case you will definitely want to be a named party. But the building and landlord cover does need to be in the owner's name as they still own the property.

Regarding general business insurance, this is up to you and speaking with a good insurance broker is essential. You will likely need to have some kind of professional indemnity insurance, possibly employer liability, public liability... the list is almost endless. There are so many different types of insurance and different requirements depending on the type of business you run that it's impossible to list them all here. I'd say, on starting out at a minimum get public liability. Professional indemnity is next! Our insurance is currently based on a letting/estate agent but tweaked slightly to fit our specific circumstances. I would make sure to mention that you are managing HMOs, as some insurance companies won't work with HMOs.

I can only give basic guidance around insurance and I can't tell you specifically what kind of insurance you will need as it does depend on the circumstances. A good broker will be able to help you.

SECTION 2:
CHOOSING YOUR AREA

SUB-TOPIC 2.1: SPAREROOM RESEARCH

Question 2.1.1: Is the house in an area that will make a good HMO?

We will dig into the Spareroom research and other types of research in this section. To get started, here are some general things to think about when starting an HMO. Some of these might be quite obvious to you and others might be a bit more thought provoking:

1. Is the house near public transport? Lots of HMO tenants don't have cars so will need a bus, train or tube stop nearby. A lot of tenants also don't want to walk very far so will choose the easiest property they can afford. 'Location Location Location', as the

saying goes. Think about where your tenants will be going (where they will work, study or pick up their benefits cheque) and then see if it is easy for them to get there from your prospective house/area.

2. Is the house near a shop? Again, as your tenants are unlikely to all have cars, you need to think about where they will get their food and day-to-day shopping. Is there a shop within walking distance? What type of shop is it? Is it a small corner shop and will that be sufficient? Is it a Lidl or a Waitrose and will your tenant type want to shop at that store? If you are planning to rent to LHA tenants, will they be happy to shop at the M&S next door or will they need to travel 20 minutes on two different buses to get to ASDA?

3. Is the house near their work? We touched on this in point 1 above, but again a lot of tenants are looking for convenience. How long will it take them to get to work? Walking is probably ideal, but a short bus ride could work as well.

4. Is the house near the city centre? Your tenants may want to have a social life. They may want to go out to dinner or to the pub. They may want to visit their friends. What else is near your HMO? If it's in a small village 20 minutes from the city centre, you may struggle to keep it fully tenanted.

5. Following on from point 4, villages probably aren't the ideal places for HMOs. You are generally looking for a place that will have enough tenants to keep your rooms filled.

6. Is the house in a safe location? It will likely depend on your tenant type as to what they consider "safe". Your LHA tenants might want to live in an area because all their friends live there, while your young professional lady wouldn't live there if her life depended on it even though it's only two blocks from her office. So make sure you know your market and what the tenants are looking for.

7. Is there enough tenant demand in the area? See the Spareroom research tips in the next question to test this. The area might meet all of the above criteria but people don't want to live there!

Question 2.1.2: How do I know if I will be able to find enough tenants?

I usually do my research using Spareroom.com. Spareroom is an amazing tool, so if you haven't checked it out already, I recommend you have a good play with it before you start your business.

In order to check the demand in an area I do the following (let's use SW11 in London as an example):

1. Go to www.Spareroom.co.uk

2. Put in the postcode for the target area (or the city) and search "Rooms for Rent"

3. On searching Rooms for Rent in SW11 there are currently 205 results

4. We then want to know how many people are looking for rooms. For this we go back to the homepage and do another search. Press "Home" and enter your postcode in the search box again. This time choose "Rooms Wanted" and press search. WOW – in SW11 there are 5,887 people looking for rooms.

5. Analyse your results. Based on this search in SW11 there are definitely more people looking for rooms (5,887) than there are rooms available (205). Your search might deliver results that are a bit less obvious. So here are some things to look for and consider:

- Not all of the "Rooms Wanted" ads might be current. Some people may have already found rooms and not removed their profile from the site.

- Not everyone looking for a room creates a "Rooms Wanted" profile. So there may be more people looking for rooms than are shown in this search.

- This search didn't drill down into the different types of rooms and prices so might be skewed if you are planning to rent to students and there are only professionals looking, or if all your rooms are going to be at the top end renting for £800 per calendar month and the people looking for rooms have a maximum budget of £600 pcm.

- Some of the people in the "Rooms Wanted" might have a very large area in their profile in which they are looking. Some may have put all of London, for instance, or all of South West London. These people may not be interested specifically in your area so might not be interested in your room.

- Consider the time of year. If it's mid-December as I do this search, there are likely a lot fewer rooms available as people tend not to move during the holidays. Or maybe it's summer, and you are looking for students to move in next month when in reality most of them have already organised their houses earlier in the year.

There are many other factors. So if your Spareroom research doesn't result in "Rooms Wanted" of at least two to three times the "Rooms Available", then you will want to dig deeper or try other areas. Use this as a rough guide to get a high level overview if this is a good area. Use common sense – if you find 500 rooms available and 10 people looking for rooms, this probably isn't the place you want to set up an HMO.

Finally, if you don't find a lot of people looking for rooms on Spareroom.com then maybe tenants in that area don't use Spareroom. Have a look at Gumtree or UPad or even

RightMove to see what is available there. Also, check out some of the other sites that I discuss in Section 5 about Finding Tenants.

Question 2.1.3: How do I know how much rent to charge for each room?

This is where you will dig a bit deeper into your Spareroom research. You'll also want to see Subtopic 2.3: Secret Shopper.

But if you've passed the high level Spareroom research and the "Rooms Wanted" exceed the "Rooms Available" (covered in the previous question), now you want to see what people are looking to pay and what other landlords are charging for their rooms. And, if you are lucky, there will be some pictures on these ads so you can get an idea of the quality of accommodation other landlords are offering.

Let's go back to the search you did in the last question – if you do the search for "Rooms Wanted" and look up in the top corner there is a link that says "Check average rents in this area".

Flatmates in SW11

This is a great tool! Click that link and you will get a list of room prices by type and area. In SW11 this could be Battersea, Battersea Park, Clapham, Clapham Junction, Lavender Hill, and London. This list separates all those by room type (double, single, bills included) and gives you an average price along with an average, min and max price. This is a really good starting point to see what other people are charging. For instance, if your rooms were going to be in Battersea and you wanted to charge £700 pcm for a double with all bills included, your room would probably rent out relatively easily as the average rate is £735 pcm for that type of room. But if you were going to charge £1,000 per month, you would be near the top-end average so it might be a bit tougher to rent out your rooms unless they are really something special!

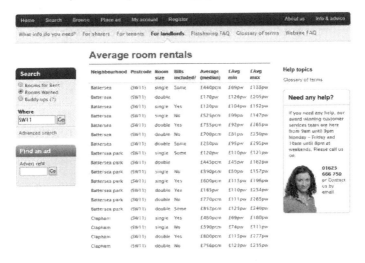

You'll also want to check the price of a one bedroom or studio flat (try Rightmove.co.uk). If one bedroom flats are renting for £550 pcm in your area, that will likely be about the maximum you could charge for a double room (all bills included). The person renting the flat would also have to pay council tax and bills on top of that. So if they downgraded to a nice double bedroom with shared kitchen and bathroom, they would save money as all the bills are included in the HMO. Most people would be unlikely to live in a shared house for the same price as they could live in their own flat.

SUB-TOPIC 2.2: RIGHTMOVE RESEARCH

Question 2.2.1: How do I know how much to offer the property owner/agent?

You should know your numbers (see Sub-topic 2.4) before you decide how much to pay the property owner and agent, but I'll give you a bit of guidance around how to determine average prices in your area to help you understand where your ballpark rent offerings should be.

With regard to average rents in the area, I would start with Rightmove. This is the biggest online property portal. Pretty much anything listed for rent online is going to be on Rightmove, so you should be able to figure out the average rental prices of properties in your area.

Let's stick with SW11 which we used previously in the Spareroom research examples.

1. Head to www.Rightmove.co.uk

2. Type in your postcode and choose "To Rent"

3. Now you can narrow down your search a bit more. Let's go through the options:

- Search radius: I normally leave it as "This postcode only" to start. But you can widen the search if you are in a smaller area or there are no results in your postcode.

- Property type: I usually start with it on "Any" as I want to be able to see both houses and flats and I can easily ignore the other stuff like "Land". But if you aren't interested in flats then by all means choose "Houses".

- Number of bedrooms: This is where you can play around a bit. I usually put a minimum of three bedrooms there and leave the maximum open. This way I can get a general idea of the prices of all the bigger houses. But if I have a specific house I'm negotiating on, and say it has four bedrooms, then I will only look at four bedroom houses in my Rightmove research. So for this example, let's use a four bedroom house as our standard so the minimum will be four and the maximum will be four.

- Price range: I leave this open because I want to get an average.

- Added to site: I usually leave this as it is. It's not really important unless there are lots of really old properties that aren't renting. But that's getting into details.

- Retirement properties: I always select "Non-Retirement Only" unless you want to start an HMO for the over 55s.

- And then the biggie – "Include Let Agreed properties". I always tick this! You want these included because these are the properties that are actually rented out so you know the price people were willing to pay for them.

4. Set your criteria as above and then choose "Search".

5. Now for our search we get a list of 45 four bedroom properties. You can see the number of results on the top, then a further breakdown by type along the left-hand side, and then your results in the middle.

6. The first thing we want to do is, near the top right corner, sort the results by "Lowest Price". We are looking to get the average for four bedroom houses,

so once we have sorted by lowest to highest price, we can start to determine the average.

7. Next, scroll to the bottom of the page to see how many pages there are. In our example there is only one page. If there was more than one page, you would want to go to the middle page and to the middle of the middle page to find the approximate "average" price… remember this isn't an exact science.

8. For our example we will scroll to the middle of the first page (because we only have one page of results). You can see by the scroll bar that I'm in about the middle of the page.

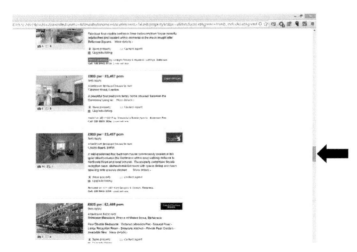

The three prices you can see here are £800, £800 and £805 per week. So that would tell me the average four bedroom house in SW11 rents for £800 pw. Now just to check, I'll scroll and have a look at the lowest and highest prices which in this area are £475 pw and £13,000 pw. WOW! Ok, this example might be a bit skewed as we obviously have a bit of luxury here... and the next most expensive is £3,500 pw... again a bit skewed. The next is £1,100 pw. We'll go with that...

With £475 as the low and £1,100 as the high, the average is £787, so we would be happy to pay about £800 pw for a normal four bed property in SW11. This is consistent with what our middle of the page results showed us. Maybe a little more for one in good condition closer to a station, and maybe a little less for one that's not so great. Dig a little deeper into each of the properties around your target price to see what the standard is and the exact area.

9. Rightmove also has a really nice map function to help with the area. If you go back up to the top in the same search and choose "Map", you'll get a nice Google Maps view with the houses in the search results marked out. If you have a specific house in mind, you can zoom into that street and see what the other houses on that street (or in the nearer vicinity) are being advertised at. Or you can look for pockets of cheaper rental areas in your wider postcode as the overall rent may be cheaper but you can still get about the same amount per room (from the Spareroom research), so those might be areas to target.

This quick Rightmove research gives you the ballpark prices you should be offering the agent/property owner. This is by no means where you should stop in your research! You need to make sure you will make a profit at those prices. So I suggest you read through to Subtopic 2.4: Knowing Your Numbers.

Question 2.2.2: What types of houses are available and will they make good HMOs?

Let's break this down into two questions.

1. What types of houses are available?

Go through steps 1 to 5 in the previous question to set up your Rightmove research. This will show you the houses available. That's easy enough. Remember, if you look on the left hand side in your search results you'll see a break down by property type (houses, detached, semi-detached, terraced, flats, etc.) and furnishing (furnished, part-furnished, unfurnished) and type of let (long-term and short-term). It will also tell you other things like parking and outdoor areas, depending on what types of properties you have and the amenities that the letting agents selected in Rightmove.

2. Will the houses in this area make good HMOs?

This is a rather broad question. There are a lot of factors governing a good HMO including location, size and layout (see the first question in this Section for a list of criteria to consider). At this point you will want to start digging down into floor plans and pictures if you want to get a Rent to Rent from an agent by looking at Rightmove. You want to make sure that the bedrooms are doubles (there may be a single here and there but generally these are much harder to rent out). You also want to make sure there are enough bathrooms. Normally, the legal requirement is one bathroom for four people, one bathroom and a separate toilet for five people, six to seven tenants need two bathrooms, one with a separate toilet. And so on. If you are going super high-end, you will want to have a higher toilet-to-tenant ratio (two to three tenants per bathroom) and maybe even a few ensuites (these are like gold dust in my area). Since you are not the owner of the house, you generally want to limit the amount of work you do to the house, so I wouldn't spend time calculating floor space to see if additional bathrooms and ensuites could be added. You ideally want something that you can get started with right away.

Let's look at the floor plan of one of the £800 pw properties from my example. In a quick overview, there is a nice patio/outdoor space, which is always a bonus (especially in London). It looks like it has a big kitchen and breakfast room so a good amount of communal space.

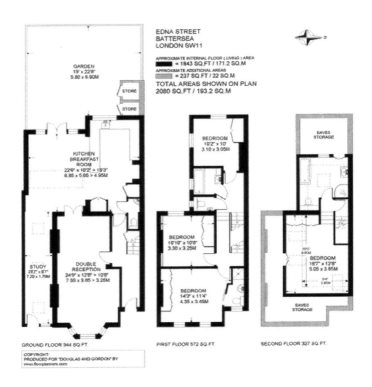

There is also a massive double reception room. I would definitely have my eye on this if I went to view the property. A stud wall and a door is quite a cheap thing to put into a property. You could easily split this room in half. The front half could be a bedroom (bedrooms must have natural light from a window). The back half could be communal space. Or it could be used as a giant bedroom. This would depend on how big the kitchen area is and how the owner feels about stud walls. (Always be upfront with the owner about something like this. You can tell them that you will put it back as it was when your lease is over so they won't even notice).

Bedrooms: In my area, if you have a decent sized communal room your minimum room size can be 6.5m^2, otherwise, if there is no communal space, it is 8.5m^2 (11m^2 and 14m^2 for a room with two occupants). In this floor plan the smallest bedroom is about 9.4m^2. So no problems there. The other three bedrooms are even bigger, with the bonus of the loft bedroom having an ensuite!

Speaking of bathrooms, there are two bedrooms with ensuites along with a full bathroom and a separate toilet in this property. That's perfect, especially if you were to add another bedroom by splitting the reception room. So three bedrooms share one bathroom and a separate toilet.

Overall, with the information we have seen so far, I think this would make a great HMO with lots of potential. Looking at the photos, the kitchen is large with a breakfast bar and table so could be used as the only living space, if desired. This depends on the type of tenant you want and the rents you want to achieve. Everything looks really nice from the pictures and it looks to be in good condition as well. This could be pretty much ready to rent out from day one. All you would need is a bit of furniture.

SUB-TOPIC 2.3: SECRET SHOPPER

Question 2.3.1: How do I know what standard my house needs to be finished to?

Secret Shopper! That's what my answer is to this question. Get out there and check out the competition. See what they have on offer. If you've gone through the questions in the previous Sub-topics you now know your target area and the target rents you want to achieve, so check out Spareroom.com, Gumtree, UPad, Rightmove and any other online portal to see what rooms are available in your target market and make appointments to do viewings as a potential tenant. Take pictures, ask the agents/landlords questions, interview the current tenants if you can. The more properties you see, the better understanding you will have for what you need to offer to get tenants flocking to your houses.

Now, your ability to do this in a discrete and believable manner may depend on what your target market is and if you can fit into that market when posing as a potential tenant. For instance, if you are 60 years old and looking to have houses full of students or young professionals, you may need to find someone to help you be a secret shopper, as it might be kind of obvious if you show up to look at a student house that you aren't planning to live there yourself. Or you could just pretend you are looking for a room for your son/daughter.

Luckily, when I originally moved to Oxford (my main investment area) I was planning to move into a shared house. I was working as a consultant and was only coming to the city on a four month contract, so I was looking for a short-term professional let with other young professionals. What I saw was ABYSMAL! I knew Oxford was a student town so I made sure I only went to look at properties which advertised themselves as "professionals only". And it may have been only professionals living in those houses, but the standard of most of those houses was no better than a very dirty and poorly kept student house. There was no sense of community, and if there was a communal area it was filled with cheap furniture with barely any light. And it was all so dirty! Every house had a dark hallway... I just remember it all being very dark. And if that is what the professionals were living in, I can't even imagine what the students live in!

Fast forward a few years to when my partner and I decided that HMOs in Oxford for young professionals was our strategy. I went and looked at a number of houses and knew that standards hadn't improved in the years since I first moved to Oxford. I'd also been on a number of courses and tours of other people's HMOs and heard that you had to have ensuite bathrooms, or big communal rooms, or no communal rooms, or fancy decor with feature walls (so many different options and conflicting advice). I was all set to start putting in ensuite bathrooms, and I spent a few hours in the paint shop looking at paint and wallpaper samples to pick feature wall colours. Then I started adding up the costs... and I started thinking about what I knew about MY MARKET. Most of my competitors' houses barely had enough lighting to even see what colour the walls were, let alone feature walls. And maybe one out of

50 rooms had its own ensuite bathroom. I thought about what stuck out to me as a young professional (my new target market) when I was looking for a house share in my target area. And I realised the house needed to be clean, fresh, and bright. And if my rooms had those qualities I would be miles ahead of the competition. Sure, an ensuite room rents out for about £50 more per week than a regular room, but I'm doing Rent to Rent and I am not spending all my money on someone else's house. I can rent a room without an ensuite just as quickly as long as it is clean, bright and fresh.

So my houses are generally painted white, which makes them feel bigger and brighter. I use coloured pillows and duvets and curtains to bring a bit of colour and excitement to a room when tenants are viewing. I have a cleaner who comes twice per month to clean the common areas so the houses never get out-of-control dirty (this is included in the tenants' rent). I have new furniture that is basic but matching so everything looks fresh. I've seen much nicer HMOs than mine, but in my market my houses are some of the nicest I've seen. I never have any problem filling rooms, even in houses with small communal areas, because I keep things fresh, bright and clean. I am miles above MY competition.

Now, I don't tell that story so that you go out and paint all your walls white and hire cleaners. That may not be necessary for your target tenant in your target market. I tell that story so that you can see how important it is to know what the competition is so that you don't waste your time and money on something that won't sell or that you could sell by doing less.

SUB-TOPIC 2.4: KNOWING YOUR NUMBERS

Question 2.4.1: Who pays for the maintenance?

I'll answer this question with another question: "Who do you want to pay for the maintenance?" This is your contract, so it's up to you and the owner to decide.

My one recommendation is that you think about your responsibility to your tenants. If something goes wrong, can you trust the owner to fix it as quickly as you would? Will his maintenance standards meet your maintenance standards? The tenants are going to be calling YOU when the shower, boiler, washing machine, fridge, door, etc. breaks. And they will keep calling YOU until it's fixed. You need to know that the owner is going to do a good job and get it done quickly. If you can't rely on him, then I suggest you do it yourself.

In most of our contracts we are responsible for all internal maintenance including the boiler and the white goods. This is because I want to make sure everything is done to my standards. A lot of the houses were a bit of a mess when we took them on, and my thoughts were that, if the property owner let the house get into a poor condition once, could I rely on him to keep things from getting that way again?

So yes, it's a bit more of a risk for us to take on the responsibility of the maintenance. We can mitigate that risk with landlord emergency insurance (covers plumbing, electrics, boiler, central heating and more depending on who you go with). And the price of this and the price of the extra risk is included in the rental amount that we offer the owner. Because we are taking on much more of the risk and doing more of the work, the owner will get less rent than if he were taking care of everything. It's a win for everyone as the owner has no hassle and a well-kept house, I know things will be done to my standards, and the tenants have their issues addressed quickly.

Question 2.4.2: What sort of ROI (Return on Investment) should I be looking for?

Everyone is looking for something different, so this should be an introspective question that you ask yourself. What return you are looking for is a personal choice. It will also depend if you have investors you are working with and need to provide them with a return or an equity stake or some other form of compensation. So know what you want and work back from there.

First, for anyone who doesn't know what ROI is - here is the calculation I use in my definition. For me it is the return on my cash invested in the deal.

Total ANNUAL profit (after all costs) / Total Cash Costs * 100 = Return on Investment

An easy way to think about what this actually means is: it is the percentage of your initial investment you will recoup in a year. So if you spend £5,000 to get the house all set up and it brings in £12,000 in rents and £6,000 in on-going costs per year (total profit of £6,000) then your ROI is 120% (£6,000 / £5,000 x 100 = 120%). So you will make all of your money back in the first year plus a bit of profit.

A lot of people are looking for 100%+ on their Rent to Rents. This means you get all of your money back within a year. Some people even get all their money back within the first month or two. This is definitely the ideal. But it isn't always possible (although if your contract term is only 12 months we recommend you get your money back as quickly as possible – don't rely on the owner extending the contract!). I'll go through some of the things you will need to spend money on later and it's different for every house. If you have a house that is already a fully furnished HMO that is up and running, it may cost a lot less than turning a three bedroom/two reception room unfurnished family home into an HMO. And it depends who your market is and what your standards are. All of these are questions that you should be starting to work out based on the previous sections of this book and your research.

We aim for 70% ROI and £100 profit per bedroom per month as a minimum for our Rent to Rents. If it meets the criteria, we will do the project. Our main target area is rather a tough one, with Article 4 (see 2.5.1 below) and Additional Licensing (so it's extremely difficult to take a family home and turn it into an HMO). Also, tenant demand is very high, so landlords who already have HMOs generally don't have problems filling their houses and rarely have voids, so there isn't a lot of room for negotiation. In your area it might be completely different, and you might be able to get a nice family home that doesn't need any painting or redecorating and just needs a few more bits of furniture and you are up and running with tenants from day one (lucky you!).

You need to step back and make a plan of what you are looking for from your property business. How much is your time worth, and how much do you need vs. how much do your investors need? 'How to set goals and understand your personal requirements' could fill a whole book on its own, so I'll just brush the surface here.

General Rent to Rent 'industry standard' is £100 per room per month minimum. Many of the people you meet who are giving talks on Rent to Rent are boasting >100% ROI, generally getting their money back within one to two months. If you can get those kinds of deals - do it! If your ROIs are a little bit lower, just make sure they meet your personal criteria. We always make sure we have a five year contract for our agreements, so if we don't make a profit in the first year we have another four years to make a profit. If your contract is only 12 months, then I would say you need to be looking for a property that pays back your investment within one to two months!

If you are working with Joint Venture (JV) partners, it's important to know who is getting what and who is doing what. The £100 per room per month minimum is the value I put on my time. If I am managing the property myself, this is the money I need to be getting to make it worth my time. Your needs might be lower, especially if you are just starting out... or they may be higher! So if we are taking on a JV partner who wants to do a 50/50 split of the profit, then the property either needs to make £200 per room per month or the JV partner needs to be managing the property and doing a bit of the work themselves. As we move to getting a lot of our properties managed by someone else, the amount I personally get from each house is lower and my time input is lower so it's win-win!

Question 2.4.3: Who pays to upgrade to HMO standards?

Depending on the size of the house (how many bedrooms, how many people, how many storeys) and what standards are expected by your council and yourself, you may have some work to do to get the property ready to rent out as an HMO.

As a minimum I would look at putting the following into any rented house:

- Interlinked smoke alarms (in the bedrooms if it's over three storeys and five people) with a heat detector in the kitchen

- Fire doors (minimum in the kitchen so that there is a clear exit route)

- Fire extinguisher and fire blanket in the kitchen

- Carbon monoxide detectors near the boilers and any other gas appliances

- Thumb turn locks on all doors that have locks

Your council may have additional requirements and most councils have a decent booklet on their website of what they expect, so have a browse. The more tenants the house will have, the more work will be required!

So who pays for these items? Well, it's up to you and the owner and your negotiation skills. Ideally, if you could get the owner to pay for everything that would be great! But more often than not you will have to cover some of these costs. Personally, we usually take on all of these costs if they are not already installed. Luckily, a lot of our houses were previously set up as licensed HMOs so they already have the fire alarms and fire doors and thumb-turn locks.

Here's a clever trick I learned from a friend. She doesn't put locks on the bedroom doors initially and tells tenants that if they want a lock on their door then they need to pay for it themselves. This way the tenant is in control. No locks means the house is more homey and comfortable, but if they want a lock, the Rent to Renter doesn't have to pay for it. Quite a brilliant idea!

That being said, we put locks on all the bedroom doors and we use a Master Key system which has a higher set-up cost but makes things much easier for us. This system means that we have one key that opens all the doors in every house so I can get in anytime and don't have to worry about carrying a bucket of keys or having multiple key safes at the houses. Also, my handyman and letting manager have their own keys, so they are always able to get in quickly to do their jobs without asking me for keys.

Make sure you include all these required (and desired) items in your numbers when calculating your expected ROI and how much you can pay in rent each month. If you are taking on a six bedroom house and need to have interlinked smoke alarms installed in each bedroom, you are looking at quite a bit of set-up costs.

Question 2.4.4: What other costs should I be aware of?

There are so many scenarios and costs that could pop up that there is no way I can provide a complete list. But here are the things we plan for at pretty much every house:

- Painting

- New carpeting (and underlay)

- Furniture

- Furnishings (plates, cups, pictures, pillows, etc.)

- Master Key System

- General maintenance (normal budget is about £500 per house for little bits and pieces here and there)

- Initial Void (depending on your area and demand and how long the set-up of the house will take. We tend to budget a month's void in the beginning just to give us some time and flexibility to fill the rooms).

Here are a few other things to think about:

- Electrical work (you should generally have an electrical certification done every five years)

- Gas Safety Check (annual)

- Travel costs (depending on how far you live from the property and how often you need to go there)

- Planning Application costs

- Building Regulation costs

- Legal fees

- HMO licensing fees

- Additional fridges

- Additional bathrooms/kitchen facilities

- Fire Safety (alarms, extinguishers, fire blankets, escape windows, fire doors)

- Junk removal

- Deposit

- Fees to letting agent (if you are renting through an agent)

- Gardener

- Cleaning

I'm sure there are many other bits and pieces that may pop up! Your first Rent to Rent will be full of surprises but a great learning experience. I learn something new with each house. Plan as well as you can and leave a bit of wriggle room with a contingency fund, be conservative with estimates, and you will be fine!

SUB-TOPIC 2.5: LOCAL RULES

Question 2.5.1: What is Article 4 and what does it mean for my HMO?

An Article 4 direction is made by the local planning authority. It restricts the scope of permitted development rights either in relation to a particular area or site, or a particular type of development anywhere in the authority's area. It requires planning permission for new development and renovations to existing buildings. And renovations can be simply changing the use from a family home to an HMO, even if you don't do any actual building work!

Article 4 doesn't just relate to HMOs. It is also used for conservation areas to encourage retention of architectural features and preserve heritage. For our purposes we will just focus on the Article 4 directive that requires planning permission to change a property from C3 (dwelling house) to C4 (House in Multiple Occupation). Normally, without a specific Article 4 directive, the change from C3 to C4 is part of the permitted development rights of a house. Many cities are taking away that permitted development right and are putting (or trying to put) Article 4 directives in place to control the number and standards of HMOs. I won't get into a debate here about whether this is right or not, but it is what is happening across the UK.

Article 4 is different from additional licensing. Planning and licensing are completely separate topics and separate departments at most of the councils. With Article 4 you need planning permission but you may not need a licence. If there is additional licensing, you need to apply for a licence but you may not need planning permission. And you may be really unlucky and need both! Licensing is covered in the next question, 2.5.2.

So, back to Article 4 and planning permission. If you are changing a house from a single family home to a shared house with up to six occupants and the house is in an area with an Article 4 directive, which removes the permitted development rights for C3 to C4 conversion, then you will need to apply for planning permission. Anything above six people is called *sui generis* in the planning world and will always need planning permission.

Most councils have their own rules about what they are looking for in the planning application. Most councils I have seen have requirements that try to ensure that there aren't too many HMOs in an area. They are also very focused on parking. It's best to speak with other HMO landlords in your area and speak directly with the council (after reading as much as possible on their website) to understand what specific things your council is looking for. You should always be aware of parking as most councils will require this, although some may waive the parking requirement if you can prove that there is easy access to public transportation or good bicycle storage in an area where a lot of people ride bicycles.

Many Article 4 directives don't cover entire councils. There may be pockets of the city that are not covered by the Article 4 directive. So it is important to research your council and your area. Most council websites have maps or lists of the areas that are covered by the Article 4 directives. You may be able to find an area or a street right next to an Article 4 area that won't require you to get planning permission. That area may have just as high a demand as the street next door which needs planning permission and plenty of hoop jumping! So remember to drill down into the detail and really know your area!

Here's a quick flowchart to help you understand if you need to apply for planning permission:

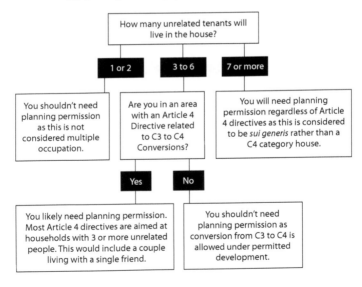

Question 2.5.2: What is additional licensing and what does that mean for my HMO?

As I mentioned in the previous question, additional licensing is different from an Article 4 directive. With Article 4 you need planning permission. You may not need a licence.

Additional licensing is brought in by councils to help ensure the quality and standard of housing in the area. Like Article 4 directives it may not cover the whole area and may just apply to specific parts of the city. So make sure you have a good browse of your council's website to understand what the licensing requirements are and where they apply.

As a start, all houses with five or more people on three or more storeys must be licensed. This is known as mandatory licensing and covers the whole of the UK. If the house you are looking at has three storeys and you are putting five or more people in it, you need a licence. If it has three storeys and only four people, you may only need a licence if it is in an area of additional licensing. The same with a house with six people but is only on two storeys – you may only need a licence if it is in an area with additional licensing requirements.

Let's have a look at the following flowchart for a high level overview if you need a licence or not:

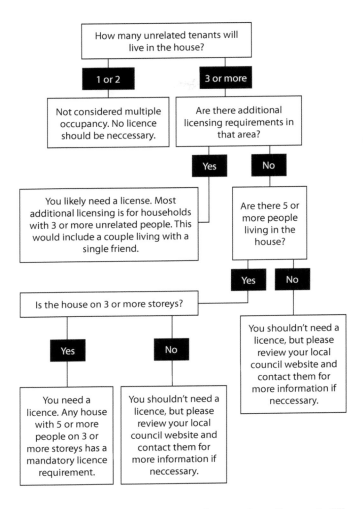

What does it mean if you do need a licence? The government has put together an excellent guide on their website (www.gov.uk/government/.../HMO_Lic_landlords_guide.pdf). Most councils also have their own guides which outline the requirements for a licensed HMO, so again make sure you check their websites and contact them for more information. Even if your HMO doesn't need a licence, it would be good to follow as many of the standards in the guide as possible as you always want to make sure you are providing quality housing that is safe! Please read the booklet as it is very informative on the requirements of an HMO.

Another great website to check out is the LACORS website. The LACORS guides are the standards (especially for fire safety) that most of the UK councils use when putting together their own guides. www.LACORS.gov.uk. If you set up your HMO to follow these guidelines, you will be at the top end of tenant safety and should meet most councils' requirements.

Each council will have their own requirements but as a high level overview the following are generally specified:

- Minimum bedroom sizes

- Minimum kitchen sizes (based on number of tenants)

- Minimum living/dining room sizes (based on number of tenants)

- Required number of toilets and showers

- Facilities offered in the kitchen relative to the number of tenants

- Requirement for safety certificates (gas safety, electrical appliances, furniture, smoke and heat alarm, emergency lighting, etc.)

Please note that licensing is very important. You can be prosecuted by the council for not holding a licence and many people have been prosecuted. You could face a fine of up to £20,000 plus costs if you do not have a licence. Also, if you are operating without a licence, the tenants (or the council if housing benefit was claimed) can apply for a rent repayment order for a maximum of 12 months' rent during the unlicensed period. So that could be A LOT of lost profits!

In most of the areas I have worked in or know others working in it is not difficult to get a licence and councils rarely decline licences unless you consistently ignore their requirements or are unsuitable as a manager of an HMO (generally criminal convictions like fraud make you unsuitable). You will have time to make any required modifications that the council recommend, and while some of these modifications can seem very petty and unnecessary they generally aren't too onerous for the professional and competent landlord who wants to provide quality housing. You can appeal the licence conditions that you don't agree with and most councils are reasonable. Mandatory or additional licensing shouldn't put you off of a property. It can mean a bit of additional work along with increased costs (licence applications and annual renewal have moderate fees), but if you are running a quality home for your tenants you should easily meet most of the criteria required as part of a licence.

Question 2.5.3: Does my council have any standards I need to meet or be aware of?

I haven't found an all-encompassing list for the councils which have Article 4 or additional licensing. This is some of the research that you will have to do on your own. And the councils are changing every day. More and more councils are trying to bring in Article 4/additional licensing and some are even getting rid of it. If I added a list now it would be outdated within weeks. So I won't even try.

My recommendation is to jump onto your council website or call your local council and find out what their requirements are and who can help. Also PIN meetings (www.pinmeeting.co.uk) are a great way to find out what is happening in your local area, as are local landlord association meetings (www.landlords.org.uk or www.RLA.org.uk). You'll be able to meet with other local investors who will be able to point you in the right direction regarding your area.

SECTION 3:
FINDING RENT TO RENT DEALS

SUB-TOPIC 3.1: HOW DO I FIND PROSPECTIVE DEALS?

This is a brilliant question. Along the lines of − is this a get rich quick scheme or do I need to actually do some work?

There are a lot of people out there selling dreams and get rich quick schemes. And there are quite a few articles written about them when the dreams collapsed around them because they didn't set up their businesses properly.

My answer to this question is that education is your shortcut. Learning from other people who have done it well and done it properly is the biggest shortcut you can find. Also, reading this book is a shortcut. And then, it's up to you to take action, get out there and do it! Put that education to use and *Just Do It* (to quote the great and inspirational Nike)!

You will also need to buckle down and do some work. Ultimately, it is a numbers game because the more houses you look at and make offers on, the more deals you will get. It's the same in all areas of property investing. The more marketing you do, the more deals you will get. Like most businesses, the more people who know about you, the more business you will get. You won't get very many Rent to Rent deals sitting at home trolling through Rightmove. You need to get out there to build relationships and look at houses. Talk to agents. Talk to landlords. Talk to anyone who will listen and tell them what you do! The more you talk and practice, the more confident you will sound and the more deals you will get.

When I started I was very unconfident. Sure, I was educated in property investing but I didn't have any experience. After I looked at 50 houses and spoke to 100 different people I was getting a lot better and could confidently answer most questions that the property owners asked. This confidence inspires more property owners and agents to be willing to work with me and makes it easier to get deals now. So I don't have to look at as many houses or talk to as many people to get a house. It's still a numbers game, the numbers are just lower.

The next few questions will break down some specific forms of marketing and targeted ways of finding the deals.

SUB-TOPIC 3.2: WHAT KIND OF ADVERTISING CAN I DO?

LEAFLETS

Question 3.2.1: Does leafleting work?

Of course leafleting works. Why do you think you get so many leaflets through your door every week? If it didn't work, every estate agent, letting agent, pizza company, etc., would stop pestering you with their flyers. But they do it and most businesses don't waste money, so it must work. Just know that it's a huge numbers game. Lots of people who are smarter than I am have done the maths and analysed their results. I've heard that you get an average of 1% response rate on leaflets. That's one person for every 100 leaflets... and that's not one deal signed, that's one person calling you! The deal rate is even lower.

So you have to be smart about this. Make sure you have a strategy. Don't just willy-nilly hand out leaflets or take 20,000 leaflets and distribute them to 20,000 houses and call it good. You need to start with a plan. Here's what I've learned in my days of leafleting.

1. Pick a small area to start with. I would say no more than 5,000 houses.

2. Be targeted. Know your area and make sure that the houses you leaflet are houses that meet your strategy and criteria.

3. Make sure these houses get your leaflets more than once. They should be getting your leaflets every four to six weeks.

4. Don't do it yourself. It's hard. Harder than I thought possible. My hands were bruised and bloodied after delivering a few of my own leaflets. Maybe deliver 500ish yourself so you know how hard it is and then hire someone! Other people may say differently – you may get to know the area better by walking around it. You can talk to the neighbours, etc., etc... but I found it gruelling, and the 500 I delivered were about my most unpleasant moments in property investing. Someone else can do it just as well – if not better – than you can!

Those are my main tips. Check the Resources section at the end of the book for my advice on where to get your leaflets.

Question 3.2.2: What should my leaflet say?

Your leaflet should be clear and concise. You need to state exactly what you are looking for.

I recommend using both sides of the leaflet. You can do black and white or colour, but no matter what you do I think it's a waste of time and effort if you don't use both sides!

On one side I put information related to a referral bonus. Most people just throw leaflets away. You might get them to read it if you can catch their attention by telling them how much money you will give them. Big writing that says "MAKE £500 TODAY" or "THIS LEAFLET IS WORTH £250" could work really well.

On the other side of the leaflet is your main message. You are looking for landlords (this is a Rent to Rent book, so that's the message we are going with).

I made the mistake early on by trying to look for people selling *and/or* renting their houses. I got very few responses because my message wasn't clear enough. Most people who wanted to sell their house didn't want to rent it out so didn't want to call, and most people who just wanted to rent their house out didn't want to get sucked into a scheme where they have to sell their house – so they didn't call either. I've found that I need to be quite specific in my marketing. I'm looking for landlords of 3+ bedroom houses who want to guarantee their rents for a certain amount of time (we say three to five years in our marketing).

For a great website to help with your leaflets I use www.smartpropertyleaflets.co.uk/ as they have some great designs and examples that you can look through. They are also reasonably priced and good quality.

Question 3.2.3: How many leaflets and how often?

People need to see your material, your brand and your message a number of times before it will stick. Different sales and marketing books talk about people needing to see your stuff five to seven times before they will call (have you ever heard of the seven points of contact?). So you can't expect people to call you after one leaflet. They will most likely just put it in the bin and never think of you again... until next time they see your leaflet and they put it in the bin again... and again... and again... but then maybe the fifth time they see it and think... "Hmmm... my sister was just talking about that" and then they throw it away. And then the seventh time they get your leaflet you are their friend, they know you, they remember you, and yes, it was their sister who was talking about this exact problem that your leaflet says it can fix! And they call. But to get the seventh leaflet to that house took 35,000 leaflets in your target area of 5,000 houses over a seven to eleven month period. So get out there and get leafleting!

Question 3.2.4: Where do I get leaflets?

Check out the Resources section! It lists who I've used for leaflets and for delivery.

NEWSPAPER ADVERTS

Question 3.2.5: What should my newspaper ad say?

This is a lot like leafleting. Be specific! You are looking for landlords who want to guarantee their rents. Your ad needs to be short and sweet. This is an example of one of our best Rent to Rent ads.

Question 3.2.6: Where should my newspaper ad be?

Do NOT put your newspaper ad in the property section, that special section where estate and letting agents list their properties. It will get lost. And most people looking in that section are looking for houses to buy or houses to rent for themselves to live in. That isn't where landlords are looking.

You want to put your ad in the classified ads. You can put it in a property section in the classifieds or under a section titled finances (or wherever else you think is best). But the classifieds is where people are looking during their browse through the news.

Also, use the free papers. Your local free paper will be one that everyone picks up and keeps around, flipping through it day after day. So you'll get access directly to Mr Everyday Landlord and Ms Accidental Landlord who are really tired of managing their own property. Maybe they've just come back from plunging a toilet or just got off the phone with a whinging tenant, and they are sitting down and relaxing to read "Your Town Weekly" and they flip through the classified ads and there is your lovely newspaper ad telling them that you can solve all of their landlord problems and guarantee their rent!

USE THE CLASSIFIEDS!

One word of warning – I made the mistake of listening to the newspaper sales person (and they are quite pushy salespeople). He upsold me an amazing banner ad on the back page of the newspaper (top of the sports section). He told me everyone would see it and that business increases by one million percent for people who put ads in these places. So I paid £500 for a few months of my ad running there. And my phone did ring a lot more often. All sales calls from people who wanted to sell me their services but NO ONE wanting to use mine! So JUST USE THE CLASSIFIEDS!

Question 3.2.7: How much should my newspaper ad cost?

This depends on (1) where you are, (2) how often the newspaper comes out, and (3) how big the distribution is. If you are in London, your ad will likely be more expensive than if you are in the Peak District. There is no set price for how much an ad costs. It will also depend if your ad is in colour and how many lines it has.

I am currently paying about £1,500 per annum for an ad in the classified in the local weekly free paper that covers my entire county. I probably could have negotiated down more but at the time I didn't realise how much leeway the sales people have. My ad is 3" x 2" and it is in colour. I'm able to change the text anytime I like by just emailing my contact at the newspaper.

A few tricks and tips. Ask how much it would be for a year, as the longer you sign up the bigger discount you get. And ask for freebies (I told the salesperson that my company wasn't VAT registered so I needed him to reduce the cost by the amount of VAT that I would need to pay)! The newspaper salesman has targets and quotas he needs to meet. He will always start at the highest price possible. I would say you can generally negotiate at least 50% off his first quote, generally more like 75% off. So use your best negotiation tactics here (like a big indrawn breath). The newspaper salesman needs you just as much, if not more, than you need him.

Also, make sure that you can change your ad whenever you need to. Make sure it's easy to change with a quick email and that you know when the deadline is to submit changes. You don't want to be stuck with the same ad that isn't working for 12 months. It shouldn't cost extra to be able to change your ad whenever you like.

NETWORKING

Question 3.2.8: Who do you know who?

Who do you know who...
is a landlord who wants to guarantee their rent?

Who do you know who...
is a landlord who is tired of being on call 24 hours a day?

Who do you know who...
wants a better return on their investment?
(Hey – you do need some funds to get a Rent to Rent up
and running... even better if they are someone else's funds.)

"Who do you know who?" is one of the most important questions that YOU can ask of EVERYONE! Who do they know who can help you with...? Whether it's finding someone who has a property they can't rent to finding the perfect builder who can build anything and doesn't charge extortionate amounts. Everyone knows someone (who knows someone) who might be able to help!

And the more people you have to put this question to, the more resources you will have available. So – as the saying goes – your network is your net worth!

Networking Events:

Do you go to your local property investor meetings? What about the local landlord associations? Do you get out and talk to people at non-property networking events? How many people know what you are doing and what you are looking for? How many relationships did you build this week? Those are just a few of the questions that I have for you when you ask me how to find more deals. So who are you asking these questions of? And how often?

I started by going to my local PIN meeting (www.pinmeeting.co.uk). I learned all I could from the local investors who attended those meetings (you can go to your first one free by using the code at the end of the book). And then I thought, these people are great because they understand what I'm looking for – but I need to meet even more people. And that's when I started to go to non-property networking events.

There I was meeting a lot of small business owners. And these are the people who are taking the time to get out and build their own businesses. Generally, people at networking meetings are going to other networking meetings and they are out meeting A LOT of people. So just by knowing them I am increasing my network into theirs. As I get to know them and build the relationship so that they like and trust me, I can start asking "Who do you know who?"

What do I say to people?

Well, at first you want to make friends. Be interested in them and what they do. You have two ears and one mouth for a reason! Use those ears to understand where the other person is coming from and what you can do to help them. Once you have built up the relationship you then ask "Who do you know who..." and then whatever you are looking for.

Networking is all about building relationships. A lot of people who go to networking events are only there to build up their businesses. You'll get to be able to identify these people quickly. You'll see them working the room taking everyone's business card and only talking about their business. They aren't listening to anyone else. They are there to sell sell sell! DO NOT be one of those people. If you get stuck with one of those people, listen and politely extricate yourself. They aren't likely to be your best source of business as they are too concerned with themselves.

I've found that the best people to meet, if you are looking for investors, are IFAs, accountants, and solicitors. These are professionals who are helping people manage their wealth. If you can make friends with them to explain how you can help them (and help their clients), then you could have a very valuable introduction to a lot of wealthy investors. It takes time to build up these relationships, so don't immediately expect the first IFA you meet to open his client book to you. They have their reputation to protect and aren't going to refer any of their good clients to you until they know you can really do what you say you can.

If you are looking for properties for Rent to Rent, these same people are your keys (as wealthy people tend to own property that will need managing). Also speak to plumbers, electricians, builders and other trades people. They are going into the houses and meeting the owners. They are likely to know which houses have tired landlords, or have listened to an accidental landlord share his woes as they fix the toilet (again)! Make friends with trades people and get them to understand exactly what you are looking for, and how you will get them more work if you get more properties, and you could have a good stream of leads coming your way.

Where to find networking groups:

Google is a great place to start! There are often a lot of local groups, even in smaller towns. There are also some bigger names out there. Here are some that I have been to:

- BNI – this is an international group with a very American structure. Only one member from each profession is allowed to go to each meeting, so you would want to be the group's go-to property guru. You would likely be competing with letting agents for a seat as they may not understand how you can work together. BNI mostly has breakfast meetings although there are some lunchtime groups.

- 4Networking – this is a national group which has a lot of meetings all around the country. Many are breakfast, but they do lunches and evening events as well. No matter where you are there should be a 4N meeting near you.

- Athena – this is for the ladies. Very similar in structure to BNI but for women only. Mostly breakfast meetings.

- British Chamber of Commerce – this is a great place to meet the local pillars of your community (and pillars of the community tend to own properties or know people who do). Mainly evening meetings.

- Business Scene – This is a group which is growing in the South West. Generally they meet in the evenings.

- Yes Group – This is a spin-off from Tony Robbins' events. A really great place to meet positive people who believe anything can happen. They often have inspirational speakers and it is a great place to get a dose of positivity and personal development and meet new people.

SUB-TOPIC 3.3: OTHER DIRECT TO LANDLORD TECHNIQUES

Question 3.3.1: How do I get direct to the property owner?

There are many ways to get directly to the property owner. I've already discussed a few in the first topics of this section:

- Leaflets

- Newspaper Ads

- Networking

I'll now cover a few more ways that I use.

Gumtree:

Many landlords who manage their own property will advertise it on Gumtree. If you scroll through Gumtree and contact those landlords with a professional message similar to the one you would use with a letting agent, you will have a good chance of speaking with them. Edit the following for what you are looking for/what their house has.

> Hello Mr/Mrs XXXX – I work as a relocation agent helping local companies house their employees. Your property looks perfect for our clients. We can provide you with guaranteed rent for up to 5 years and we take care of all of the maintenance and tenant management. If this sounds like it could be of interest to you, please contact me at XXXXX.

Direct Mailing:

You may have heard people talk about the "HMO List". They normally mean the list of licensed HMOs from their local council. Remember our discussion from Sub-topic 2.5 when we talked about additional licensing and mandatory licensing? All HMOs that need a license must apply to the council, therefore the council will have the details of all those properties and their owners. Depending on the technological capabilities of the council, this list may be hard or easy to come by. Some councils will simply send you a list via email; with others you may have to go to the council office and write down each name and address from a hardcopy (I know people who have done this). However your council does it, ALL councils are required to provide this information if you ask for it. It will not have the owner's phone number, but it will have at a minimum the owner's (or manager's) name and the address of the property. Many will also have the address of the owner/manager. Ideally you will get the latter address, as this way your letter will go directly to the property owner. But if you only get the property address, don't despair! You can still send your letter, but you just need to put something on the outside of the envelope to make sure the tenant knows to pass it on to their landlord. Something as simple as "Private and Confidential" or "Urgent information for the home owner" should help. I've had many property owners contact me from a letter which has gone to their tenants and been passed on.

Question 3.3.2: What should I say to the property owner?

Make sure you start with how what you are proposing benefits them. Like all sales, you need to tell them how you can solve their problems! Maybe they don't even know they have a problem... so that's where I would start.

1. Build Rapport. You want to be in a long-term business relationship with this person. I've mentioned it before that trust is a huge thing. While you want them to get to know and like and trust you so they will sign your contract, you also want to get to know them to ensure you can like and trust them as well. Spend some time building the relationship and understand who they are and what they are looking for. Not all landlords hate their tenants and hate plunging toilets (although lots do); some may hate their letting agent, some may be moving overseas and no longer able to manage themselves. So sit down, have a cuppa and get to know them, which leads on to number 2...

2. Find their pain. Now that you are friends focus on their pain. Find out why they are talking to you.

Something must have got them to respond to your advertising. If they hate plunging toilets, then remind them a few times during the conversation about how much trouble tenants are and how you will answer all the late night phone calls and how Mr Owner will sleep comfortably and never have to plunge another toilet. Or maybe they hate their current letting agent. This is where you make sure you sympathise (never bash the agent... that's just tacky) and discuss the benefits that you can provide above and beyond their agent. Understand where their current agent is letting them down and how you can do better. Maybe the agent found the last tenants – who trashed the house. Explain your system of checking the house every month/quarter to ensure everything is in good condition, or explain your excellent referencing criteria and thorough checks. Mr Owner's property will be safe in your hands and he won't have to worry about a thing with you in charge. Leading to number 3...

3. Focus on the benefits. This is one of the top tips in every sales book I've ever read. Don't tell them what you can do, tell them how that benefits them. Don't tell them that you will take all the midnight phone calls. Tell them they will never have to answer a tenant phone call in the middle of the night ever again. Don't tell them that their current agent sucks... tell them that the house will stay in top notch condition and grow in value under your care.

So that's it... be the owner's friend, push his pain button, and then show him the picture of what his life could be like with you solving all his problems.

Question 3.3.3: How can I get the property owner to accept that I would be putting multiple tenants in instead of one family?

Similar to the previous question, make sure you understand what the owner is looking for. If you can solve his problem, does it matter how many tenants you will have living there?

Try not to focus on the number (or type) of tenants, but on how you are benefitting him and how he doesn't have to worry about it. He will get his property back in the same or BETTER condition. You are the owner's friend now and he trusts you, so just focus on the benefits. He doesn't have to take care of the tenants as you will do all of that. You are his "tenant" and that's easy enough as there is only one of you!

This may be harder depending on your market. For instance, if you are renting to young professionals who are at work all day as lawyers and doctors, it may be a bit easier to tell the owner that they won't cause any problems and there will be much less wear and tear than if he had a normal family with their 2.4 children and their dog running around in the house.

If you are in the LHA (benefits) tenant market, it may be a harder sell. This isn't my area of expertise so I don't know all the pros and cons, but I'm sure if you explain your management and tenant-find process and how you can take care of everything and solve the owner's problem, it will be fine. And you must tell the owner what type of tenant you will have because there can be insurance (and even mortgage) impacts with some types of tenants, like LHA tenants.

This is why it is so important to find the property owner's problem. It's hard to sell your services without knowing why someone was considering buying them in the first place! But just stay positive and assure the owner that no matter how many tenants are living in his house, you are the only person he will have to deal with and you are responsible and will manage all the hassle so that he just has to cash his monthly pay cheque.

Question 3.3.4: How can I answer the question: "What makes you say that you can guarantee the rent for XX number of years?"

Yes, this is a big question. Ultimately the property owner is asking, how can you guarantee the rent?

You've done the research (Section 2) so you know the demand in the area and the supply of other houses. You know what your target tenant market is looking for and you know that you can provide that to them with this house. Be strong, be confident. Don't give away all your secrets but tell him that you've done the research, that you've got a couple of properties already, or that you have been working with someone who does. He is just looking for ways to ensure he can trust you.

Personally, I work with young professional tenants. I talk to owners/agents about how I work directly with the companies that employ these young professionals and I tell them that we have a huge list of potential tenants and that we have never struggled with demand. This means that we always get our rent and therefore we can always pay the owner's rent.

If you are really struggling to convince the owner, you may be able to get rent guarantee insurance. I've been able to have my limited company credit checked (by the NLA) and the owner can purchase rent guarantee insurance for under £100 per year to cover any default by me. You will need to have a company which has been going for a few years to make this work. Otherwise, you can tell the owner that there will be rent guarantee insurance on all the tenants you will be putting in. I would only use this as a last resort if you haven't built up quite enough rapport and trust on their side but you still really want the house. I've only had to get insurance on one property and I was happy to do that because I knew, once he saw he could trust me, he would pass over his other properties for me to manage as well!

SUB-TOPIC 3.4: USING AGENTS

Question 3.4.1: How should I approach letting agents?

Letting agents can be a tough nut to crack. Many of them are uninterested in doing things differently. This is especially true at some of the larger branches or big chains. The bigger chains will also have big legal departments which won't like people using any other contract but their standard contract. So you may want to start with the smaller, independent letting agents until you are comfortable talking to agents and have some proof of concept in the form of other Rent to Rent properties you can show them.

How do you approach the agent? I tend to find a property on RightMove that meets my criteria and then contact the agent with a message like:

> Is this property still available? I am a relocation agent who works with companies in the local area to house their employees. We are looking for a number of properties similar to this to rent out on long-term agreements. Is this something that the owner might be interested in? Do you have any other similar properties that this may be suitable for?

This should generate a call from the agency, or at least an email response. You can also send a message to all the letting agents with properties currently available on RightMove (after you have done a search, scroll to the very bottom for the message area). Again, use a similar message:

> I am a relocation agent who works with companies in the local area to house their employees. We are looking for a number of large properties with three or more bedrooms to rent out on a long-term basis. Do you have any properties that this may be suitable for?

The agent who responds to your message may not be the main decision maker at the company (unless it is one of the small independents). So if you are speaking with someone at a larger agency, you may want to try to get the name of the letting manager or office manager to set up an appointment to speak with him.

The other option is to just book a viewing and then discuss your requirements with the person who shows you around. They should be able to tell you about other properties and also give you the name of their boss if they are unable to make decisions themselves.

Rather than sending a generic message, you can pop into the different branches (although this will miss some of the smaller independents as they will be online companies only). Ask to speak with the lettings manager. You may need to make an appointment in advance.

Question 3.4.2: What do I say to lettings agents to secure suitable properties?

Don't be afraid to move slowly. You may not get everything across to the lettings agents the first time you meet and they may not pass you all of the best rental properties on their books immediately. Property is a relationship/people business. So make sure you build your relationships and create a firm foundation.

You want to make sure the agent understands what's in it for them. They generally get paid one or all of the following:

- Tenant find fee from the landlord

- Admin/Reference fee from the tenant

- On-going management fee

- Mark-up on repairs and maintenance.

So if you are speaking to the letting manager or the office manager, make sure they understand that they will still get paid by the owner for any initial tenant find fees and management fees that they are already contracted to receive. And then let them know that the management fee they are getting is going to be effortless as you will be managing the property so the tenants will be calling you with problems, not them.

Try not to dwell on the fact that the agent will be losing out on the tenant referencing fee going forward. Make sure to tell them that you will be paying your fee and are happy to be referenced, but as you will be signing a long-term agreement they won't be getting any on-going referencing fees. Although you can agree something else with them if you like.

The biggest thing is to make sure that they understand that they will still be "managing" the property in the eyes of the owner and will still be entitled to whatever management fee they have agreed with the owner. You aren't there to steal that fee away from them – you are there to make their management easier.

If you are speaking with a general agent (not the manager), they will get a commission based on the number of properties they let out. So their main concern is whether you really can rent this property and they will be really excited if you say you want to take on more than one property. You could be the easiest commission they earn! But be wary of this excitement and make sure that you don't go viewing every property on their books because they think it's great, but as they haven't spoken to their boss – who is the decision maker – he immediately vetoes your proposal because you didn't get to know him as well.

SECTION 4:
MANAGING A LIGHT REFURBISHMENT

SUB-TOPIC 4.1: STANDARDS AND REQUIREMENTS

Question 4.1.1: What legal requirements do I have to comply with (smoke alarms, fire doors, etc.)?

There is no one answer to this question. This will depend on the size of the house, how many people are living in it, what your council licensing requirements are and what your council's requirements are in general for rental properties.

Even if the council doesn't require anything, I would say, at a minimum for the safety of your tenants, you would want:

- Interlinked smoke alarms in the hallways (highest points) and a heat detector in the kitchen

- Thumb turn locks on all doors so that tenants can get out of the house without needing a key

- Fire doors on all entrances to the kitchen

- Clear exit (which doesn't go through the kitchen) from any bedroom (in case of a fire). So if you have a bedroom off the kitchen, make sure the window will open to allow escape without having to go into the kitchen to reach an external door.

If your house has three or more storeys and five or more people, it will fall under mandatory licensing rules. The government has put together a good guide called "The Licensing of Houses of Multiple Occupation in England" (www.gov.uk/government/.../HMO_Lic_landlords_guide.pdf).

While this guide doesn't give specifics on what exactly you need to have in your house to meet HMO criteria, it walks you through understanding if it is an HMO and what the licensing requirements are, through to what happens if you don't get a licence. It's a good guide for a beginner HMO landlord to have a read through.

If you want to see the minimum national standards for HMOs, then the RLA (Residential Landlord Association) has a good summary of these in their "Housing Act Guide: Minimum National Amenity Standards for Licensable

HMOs" (www.rla.org.uk/landlord/guides/housing_act/docs/all/minimum_national_amenity_standards_for_licensable_hmos.shtml).

This guide shows the number of bathrooms, kitchens and other facilities required. It is a good minimum standard to follow.

Most councils have their own guides setting out what they require in a licensed HMO. These are generally good standards to follow even for unlicensed HMOs. Also, if there is additional licensing in an area, the council will have their own rules about the minimum standards required. So make sure you check your council's website or speak directly to your council's HMO licensing department. This department will be separate from the planning or building regulations department.

Finally, there is the LACORS guide (www.rla.org.uk/docs/LACORSFSguideApril62009.PDF). This guide is used as the standard for many councils across the UK and focuses on fire safety. If you have a read through, it will give you a lot of ideas on how to make your rental properties safer. You can apply these ideas to your own home to make it a safer place as well. Some of the tips are eye opening!

Question 4.1.2: Where do I go to obtain a list of health and safety requirements for HMOs?

Your local council will be able to provide you with the specific requirements in your area. There are minimum national standards, which the RLA sets out nicely here: www.rla.org.uk/landlord/guides/housing_act/docs/all/minimum_national_amenity_standards_for_licensable_hmos.shtml. Your local council should have a guide which states what is necessary in your specific area. This is especially true for areas with additional licensing. All councils can increase the requirements from the minimum national standards if they so choose. I think it is best to follow the minimum standards that your council recommends, even if you don't have to. This is both for the safety and comfort of your tenants, who are your customers, and also because your competition will be following those minimum guidelines. If you want to have a full house, you need to provide quality accommodation. There may be times when some of your council's requirements may not fit with your specific house. In this instance it is worth working with the council to come up with a plan to get around this, whether it is for a longer time period to implement a solution or to find another solution to the problem. I've found that if you speak to the right person, they are often willing to help, as you are both working towards providing a safe house for the tenants.

Question 4.1.3: Who is responsible for the gas safety check?

This is something you should agree ahead of time with the property owner. It is a legal requirement to have a gas safety check done annually and a certificate completed.

I take out the British Gas Landlord Emergency Cover on all of my Rent to Rent properties (there are similar companies which provide similar cover). Included in the price of this is the annual Gas Safety Certificate. I generally provide the certificate for all of my houses as a bit of a bonus for my property owners. It's also easiest for me to do it because I am managing the day-to-day running of the house and am able to get in and out quite easily, whereas the owner needs to give me 24 hours' notice before he comes in. I've found that if I arrange the gas safety certificate myself, it's easier and adds a little bit of higher level service to my property owners.

Question 4.1.4: Do both the property owner and the Rent to Renter need to get an Energy Performance Certificate (EPC)?

No, only the house needs an EPC. If the house was rented before, then the owner will have got an EPC and you can use that one.

You may want to consider getting a new EPC if you have done a significant amount of work, such as putting in new loft insulation, adding extra bathrooms, or putting in double glazed windows, etc. But normally this won't be necessary.

To see if a house has an EPC, you can go to www.EPCregister.com to search.

N.B., the government has brought out minimum standards which will come into effect in 2018. As there is constant talk of bringing those standards in sooner and making them stricter, keep your eye on changing government legislation in this area.

Question 4.1.5: How much should I spend refurbishing?

The ideal Rent to Rent property needs little to no refurbishment. Or that is what we have all been told. In our area when we were starting out the properties we took on tended to be pretty run down and needed some love and attention. So we had to come up with some rules and structure to determine how much we could and would spend fixing up a property which we didn't own.

Prices are different throughout the country. For those of you "up north" your labour costs for painting and maintenance will generally be a lot lower than "down south". I won't go into specifics on exactly how much you should spend. Rather, I'll refer you to Section 2: Choosing Your Area and Sub-topic 2.4: Knowing Your Numbers. There is a question there about what sort of ROI to be looking for. I think this is the key metric to determine how much you should spend on refurbishing a property.

Refurbishment can be anything from a lick of paint to a full remodel and ripping out of bathrooms and putting in ensuites. Generally, for a Rent to Rent, we wouldn't recommend doing as much as if you had bought the property. Things can always happen, people can change. For instance, you might spend £30k on a refurbishment because you've got the lease for 10 years, but then after two years you are bored of the property and or that property doesn't fit into your portfolio any more but you still haven't made back your initial cash input so you are stuck. Or the owner might have a life changing situation and need the property back. We are all human and we like to create win-win situations. While I don't recommend having a break clause in your contract for the property owner, you also don't want to force someone into bankruptcy because you can't cancel the agreement. So basically, just be sensible. I like to call it a light refurbishment. The biggest refurbishments I've done with a Rent to Rent is rip out a bathroom suite which was falling apart, doing a garage conversion (split 50/50 with the owner) and turning a living room into an ensuite bedroom. All of these met our ROI criteria.

So focus on ROI and use the actual £££ amount as a sense check.

Question 4.1.6: Do I need planning permission?

This depends on the area your house is in and what the council requires.

Normally the following applies:

- a single family home, for planning, is category C3 – Dwelling House

- a home with three to six unrelated people sharing is category C4 – House in Multiple Occupation

- a house with seven or more unrelated people sharing is called *sui generis* for planning purposes

Conversion from C3 to C4 is normally included under permitted development. To move from either (or any) category to *sui generis* requires planning permission. So if you will have more than seven people in the house you will always need planning permission.

Article 4 is the statute which takes away the permitted development rights from C3 to C4 (Article 4 directives can do other things so check with your council what type of Article 4 directive they have in place). See questions 2.5.1 for more information on Article 4 directives.

Question 4.1.7: Do I need building regulations approval?

There are lots of ways of doing things regarding building regulations (if only all these questions could have simple answers). The following are some general guidelines to help you understand what your requirements are, but there are some grey areas and it's up to you to discuss this with your council/solicitor/property owner to understand the risks and make a decision.

1. If you do work on the property – like new bathroom, building walls, changing electrics – then you need building regulations approval. A Rent to Rent is just like any other property in that way. So if you are doing work, you likely need building regulations approval.

2. If you aren't doing work, and the property was already an HMO and you really don't do any work (no new smoke detectors, no locks on the doors, etc.) then you shouldn't need to get building regulations approval. If the owner made any changes then they would have been the ones to make the building regulations application and any issues would be down to them to sort out.

3. This last one is something to watch out for. If you are putting locks on the individual bedroom doors, you may need building regulations approval. Some councils are pickier about this than others. By putting locks on the doors you may be creating a "bedsit" type HMO rather than just a shared house HMO. This can be considered a material change of use to "rooms for residential purposes". This can be the

case even if you don't put kitchen or ensuite facilities into the bedrooms. Some councils will require a full building regulation application for the change of use, which will require additional costs and could require additional work depending on what the inspector decides. So be careful. Again, I've not heard of this happening in many cases but some councils are watching out for this. Other councils couldn't care less about policing this type of thing right now.

Be aware of what the risks are. I would always recommend submitting the correct application and getting the building regulations approval as required by your council! It is probably best to pop along to your local property investors meeting and see what other landlords in your area are doing.

SUB-TOPIC 4.2: FINDING THE RIGHT TRADES PEOPLE

Question 4.2.1 Do I need an architect?

Generally, no, you don't need an architect. I once heard a great planning consultant speak and she seemed to be vehemently opposed to using architects in most cases. And with a Rent to Rent you shouldn't be doing any significant building work, since even an extension would probably be a bit ambitious in a Rent to Rent property, so I wouldn't think there would be occasion for an architect.

You may need some drawings done, like floor plans or even moving around a bathroom or putting up a stud wall. This generally doesn't require an architect to draw up the plans. Most builders can do simple plans and even interior decorators can make floor plans using very accurate software. If you think about it, if you just want some floor plans for your advertising, letting agents and estate agents, don't hire architects for their floor plans. You can even make them yourself using simple, common software if you are technologically minded.

So I would say, steer clear of architects unless you are doing development projects!

Question 4.2.2: How do I find a builder/ handyman/tradesperson?

Finding trustworthy and reliable trades people was one of our biggest challenges starting out!

In the beginning I went to a lot of local networking meetings. Under Section 3: Finding Rent to Rent Deals, I talk a bit about networking. Networking groups are where I found the first trades people I used – from decorators to handymen. It worked well as most of them came recommended from others in the group. They did great work but they were also more established, and the problem with these tradesmen who were out networking, they were extremely busy... and generally added a premium to their price tag because they had a lot of work and were in demand.

I just didn't feel like I was going to get the service I needed using these busy tradesmen. After all, I could sign a contract and take on a house within a couple of days or weeks. If it needed painting, then I needed to have someone who could paint it with very little notice because I couldn't leave the house sitting untenanted while waiting for trades people.

I'll admit I stressed for quite a while about this. I scoured the internet and all the "Trust a Trader" type websites and put up projects and tried to get quotes, but it was a mess and took a lot of time.

Then I remembered my local PIN meeting and realised there are other investors in my area and I knew that they would have trades people they liked. I can't urge you enough to get to know investors in your local area. They may be your competition but most of the property people I've met at networking meetings are really helpful! I sent a desperate message to my local PIN host and within minutes had the name and phone number of the builder/handyman that she used. I knew she was experienced and had done a lot of refurbishment so if they were good enough for her they would be good enough for me. And luckily, they were also just getting started with their own company, so they didn't have a huge client list. In fact, my main handyman/builder/do-it-all guy is about 20 years old and he's amazing! He has property maintenance experience and knows how to do pretty much everything. And if he doesn't know how to do it, he knows someone who can. He's local and knows everyone and everything. It's perfect! And it was as easy as asking some of the local investors in my area who they use.

Question 4.2.3: Who do I need on my team?

Your team will be dependent on your size and how many properties/tenants you have.

To start with you only need you! Just get out there and get going.

The next person you need is the reliable handyman (see the

previous question). This is someone who can be available at any time to get to the house if a toilet needs plunging or something breaks. This is for your general day-to-day maintenance. Bigger maintenance should either be the property owner's responsibility or you should have some kind of emergency landlord cover (we use British Gas).

Once we got past three HMOs that we were managing on Rent to Rent agreements, I found that most of my time was spent doing tenant viewings. This was not an efficient use of my time, so the next person we got on our team was a letting manager. She is responsible for responding to messages on Spareroom and via email from tenants interested in renting a room from us. She then does all the viewings and leads them through the process until they pay their admin fee, at which point they are turned over to referencing. Just as a side note: I found our first letting manager at our local PIN meeting. We met at PIN and became friends on Facebook. When I posted a message on Facebook saying that I was looking for part-time help, she responded and it was perfect. She wanted to learn the business and was very personable and outgoing. Remember, this is a key member of your team. They need to be able to build rapport and make people want to rent your room and they also need to be able to tell a good tenant from a bad tenant. I would suggest that you don't have just anyone doing your viewings as the letting manager is one of the first points of contact with potential tenants.

Once we got to 8+ properties it was time for a property manager. I had been doing pretty much everything (except the handyman work and tenant viewings) myself. At this point I was only spending about two hours a day managing the properties and tenant issues, but I found it quite stressful. I think I'm a bit too nice to be a landlord, and any tenant problem, even made-up ones, really upset me. So I needed someone between me and the tenants. The property manager took over the mobile phone that the tenants called when they have problems and took over the day-to-day management of the handyman, tenant changeover, tenant viewings, referencing, etc. Basically the property manager is the person working IN my business while I am the person working ON my business, and working ON the business is where building the wealth comes from!

Another person you can look to add to your team is a great admin person. I have used a number of Virtual Assistants (VAs) over the years for both my property business and other businesses. For easier tasks I tend to hire off-shore VAs through Elance.com. For more detailed work or things that are more important I use a UK Virtual Assistant company. This book isn't about hiring people so I won't go into all the details about hiring and working with Virtual Assistants, but look into it. They are amazing!

SUB-TOPIC 4.3: INTERIOR DESIGN TIPS

Question 4.3.1: What is the right standard?

The right standard depends on your tenant and your competition. If you've followed the guidance in Section 2: Choosing Your Area, you will have scoped out the competition and know what standard you need to maintain to be a step ahead of them!

Question 4.3.2: I have heard you should dress a house. What does that mean?

Dressing a house is simply making it look pretty and homey for potential tenants who come on viewings. When I have a new house that I am trying to fill I always make sure everything is as neat and tidy as possible and pull out my "staging kit". This is full of duvets and pillows and flowers and lamps, i.e. all the things that make a room feel like home. This way your tenant isn't walking around looking at bare mattresses and bare walls. It adds some colour so they can visualise actually living in the room.

At a minimum I would suggest that you put some duvets and nice covers and pillows on the beds. They don't have to be expensive and you can reuse them over and over.

I put pictures on the walls which I leave in place – just cheap canvas prints from B&M Bargains (I love B&M Bargains).

I also try to make the table look nice. I set it out with some dishes, cutlery and wine glasses, and maybe put some flowers in the centre. Have dish towels hanging nicely on the rails. Again, put pictures on the walls.

If there is a shared living room I put down some throw pillows. I try to include a nice rug if the floor isn't carpeted, and put more canvas pictures on the walls. Those few pictures are an easy and cost effective way to really liven up a room and make a house feel homey.

Once you've dressed the house take lots of pictures. I use these as my stock photos of the rooms and the house for all advertisements. The next time you advertise the room there will be a tenant living in it. And they are never going to be as neat and tidy as your staging photo. So make sure you can show future tenants how nice the house can look!

Question 4.3.3: What furniture and other items should I include with my HMO?

Unlike single lets, I believe all HMOs should be fully furnished. HMOs are generally used by more transient tenants. Whether they are young professionals or work-hardened labourers, the tenants are generally not planning on living in the HMO permanently and generally won't be bringing a houseful of furniture with them.

Bedrooms should be furnished with:

- Bed and bed frame (I recommend a metal bed frame that is sturdy and open underneath for additional storage space for the tenant)

- Wardrobe

- Chest of drawers (sometimes I buy a wardrobe or gent's robe that has built in drawers if the room is a bit small)

- Bedside table

- Curtains

Kitchens should have all the necessities for cooking and eating:

- Enough fridges so that each tenant can have a minimum of one shelf in the fridge and one in the freezer

- Kettle

- Toaster

- Microwave

- Dish Towels

- Dish Drainer

- A set of frying pans and a set of sauce pans

- A knife set

- Cutting Boards

- There should be at least one of the following for each tenant:

    - Plates

    - Cutlery (knives, forks, spoons, teaspoons)

    - Glasses

    - Coffee Mugs

- A table and enough chairs so that each tenant can have one (the table might be in an adjoining room and, if space is tight, chairs can be folding chairs kept in storage when not used)

- Window Coverings (blinds/curtains)

Living Rooms should have:

- Sofa or other comfortable seating

- TV (with freeview or Sky/Virgin depending on the standards in your area)

- Curtains

That isn't an exhaustive list, but it gives you the basics of what is required for a standard HMO.

Question 4.3.4: Where do I get all these things from without spending a fortune?

In the Resources section you will find some additional information, but for now I'll say B&M Bargains! If this store is local to you, GO THERE. I buy as much as I can from B&M and I love it. It's cheap but cheerful. It's maybe not the right quality if you are super high-end, but generally everything is serviceable, and while it may wear out faster (I'm thinking of the £3 set of three frying pans) it is cheaply and easily replaced. I get pretty much all my staging gear from here along with most of the stuff to kit out the kitchen.

For cheap toasters, kettles and microwaves I go to ASDA or Wilkinsons and get their own brand. It's generally a fiver for a kettle and a toaster and under £50 for a microwave. Again, I load up on lots while I'm there as they do value priced dishes and cutlery as well.

For furniture I've tried IKEA, but it isn't very close to where I am and it's a pain to build it all. I also tried ordering from Tesco and ASDA and both really let me down and weren't able to deliver my order on the day they promised (a total nightmare ensued as tenants were moving in the next day). So now I use Let Us Furnish which is a Welsh furniture supplier which specialises in Buy-to-Let and HMO furniture packs. The furniture is good quality and not flat packed. Everything comes already built and the delivery team puts it exactly where I want it and takes away all the packaging! It's so easy AND they deliver nationwide. It might come at a slightly higher price than IKEA, ASDA, or Tesco but the level of service is second to none and has saved me days of hassle! They also have plans for a rental furniture line specifically for Rent to Renters. This way you wouldn't have the huge upfront cost of furniture but could spread it with your monthly bill payments. Brilliant! Check the Resources section for their website and contact details.

SECTION 5:
TENANTS

SUB-TOPIC 5.1: FINDING TENANTS

Question 5.1.1: What are the different advertising options to find tenants?

Most letting agencies use RightMove.co.uk to advertise for tenants. Zoopla is also popular and there are a few others. I've found these are not so good for room only rentals, in my area at least.

There are some specific sites which are for HMOs let by the room and these generally work much better for the type of tenant you may be looking for. Your advertising will depend on the type of tenant that you choose. If you are gearing towards LHA tenants who may not spend a lot of time online, then newspaper ads may be your best form of advertising.

Gumtree can be a good option. A lot of people go there for general browsing. I haven't had a lot of luck with Gumtree in my area as I find the people looking on that site aren't in the higher end of the price range that my houses demand, but Gumtree ads do generate some interest.

I mainly use Spareroom.co.uk for all of my advertising. It's easy to place an ad and a lot of people use the site. You can add pictures and videos and unlimited text. It easily leads you through all the information you need to place an effective ad. Other competitors include Upad.com and Easyroommate.com, which are both very similar. Try them all and see what works in your area.

Finally, I have my own website. Once you have a few houses it may be worth advertising on your own website. I also do a bit of data capture on my website which means potential tenants can sign up to my list to be "the first to know when we have a room available". This way, as soon as we know a room will be vacant, I can send them a newsletter which will direct them to our website so they can see more pictures. This works really well because when someone is living in a house share they tend to keep looking for a new room every 6-12 months. Also, they will generally know other people living in house shares who will be looking for rooms. It helps keep you at the front of their minds when they get an email from you every few weeks/months with the newest rooms available.

Question 5.1.2: What tips and tricks do you have to remain competitive so tenants take your room?

I think it's all about knowing your competition. Every once in the while get out there and pick a couple of rooms that are advertised on Spareroom or Gumtree and set up viewings. Pose as a tenant (or if you wouldn't fit the tenant criteria, pose as the potential tenant's parent or colleague looking for a place for a child/co-worker just moving into the area). Check out what the other landlords in your area are doing. This is the best way to make sure you stay on top.

Also, I think it's key to have someone who is personable doing the tenant viewings. Frankly, I was rubbish at it. I'm a bit introverted and tended to just let the tenants wander around on their own. You want someone with people and sales skills. They need to make friends with the tenant and sell the room. The person doing the viewings is the potential tenant's first contact at your property. You want them to feel comfortable with that person so that they are comfortable in your property.

Finally, have good pictures of the rooms all dressed (see the last Section under Interior Design Tips, Sub-topic 4.3). If you aren't filling the house for the first time, you are likely to show the room with the current tenant's belongings in it. And that tenant may be a bit messy so the room might not look its best. But the photos which you have on your ad and your website should be of the room at its best so that the tenant can visualise a cosy home.

Question 5.1.3: Should I mix tenant types?

Generally no, you shouldn't mix tenant types. From Section 2: Choosing Your Area you should know what kind of tenants you want to rent to and you should stick with that. People will stay longer if they feel comfortable in your HMO. And they will feel more comfortable if they are with other people who are like them. So if you are renting to young professionals, don't put any students in the property. If you are renting to DSS tenants, your young professionals probably won't like the vibe.

SUB-TOPIC 5.2: REFERENCING TENANTS

Question 5.2.1: What types of reference checks should I do?

This depends on your tenant type. At a minimum you need to get the following:

- **Photo ID** – and make sure that it really is them. If you aren't doing the viewings, make sure that the person who does the viewings can confirm that the person in the photo is the person they met, and make sure that is the person who moves into the room on moving day!

- **Recent payslip**. This will show you both that they have a job and are getting paid (and you can match it to their bank statements). It will have their **National Insurance Number** (this way you can chase them and get a CCJ, a County Court Judgement, if they stop paying or do a runner).

- Three months **bank statements** to skim through

just to make sure there are no unusual transactions that you wouldn't like someone living in your house to be making. Or to make sure they don't have a huge negative balance. You can also check that they really do have an income coming into their account.

I would also recommend that you check with their employer to confirm their salary and confirm with a previous landlord that they were a decent tenant. A lot of people say that you should check with the landlord before their most recent one, because if they are a bad tenant the current landlord might say they are great just to get the tenant out of their house! So take landlord references with a pinch of salt!

Lastly, you should run a quick credit check on the tenant. There are a number of companies online who do this (but you must have your tenant's permission). This way you can see if they have outstanding CCJs or major credit issues.

Question 5.2.2: Should I do the reference checks myself or rely on another company?

When I started I did a lot of reference checks myself. I used a company called Letting Ref which was great. It was free to gather all the tenant's information. I would put their first and last name along with their email address into Letting Ref and then the tenant would get an email asking them to fill out all the other relevant information (employment info, previous landlord, etc.). The site has a great script with a list of questions to use when contacting the landlord and employer, and it was really easy to track everything. And, best of all, it was free! The only thing you needed to pay for was a credit check, which was about £10. So it was really reasonable and great for the DIYer.

Now, I'll admit that I hate talking on the phone and calling round to all the employers and previous landlords. So I've switched to the NLA's (National Landlord Association) referencing service. I'm an NLA member so I get a discount (you get lots of other great benefits for being a member so I highly recommend it). They do all the calling and chasing for you. Again, like Letting Ref, you simply give them the tenant's full name and email address and away they go. You can also buy rent guarantee insurance for tenants (or guarantors) who pass the referencing.

Speaking of guarantors, should you use them? I know some investors make all tenants have a guarantor. This is a great idea, but I'm a bit soft hearted. So if a tenant can pass the referencing on their own I don't make them get a guarantor. But if they are new to the country or didn't pass the credit check, they must have a guarantor. The ideal guarantor is a UK homeowner... but I've also used overseas parents for tenants who are coming on work placements. I figure (and I haven't been proved wrong so far) that if the tenant has a company sponsoring them to come to the UK, the company will have done a thorough interview and feel that they are a decent person. So I just make sure I have their parents' contact details and a signed guarantor form and sometimes a double deposit, and just go with the flow.

Question 5.2.3: I have a tenant from overseas. What do I do?

I touched on this a bit in the last question. Ideally, the tenant will have a guarantor in the UK who is a homeowner. I've found that often this isn't possible.

I work with young professionals so what I tend to do is either take a double deposit and/or two months' rent upfront and/or have their parents sign a form as a guarantor. Most of my tenants from overseas are coming on a six month work placement. So I assume the company has done a good interview as they are sponsoring the tenant, and generally these tenants are coming from good schools and good backgrounds. And while people can do a runner no matter what their background, generally these tenants are reasonably responsible (i.e. slightly 'nerdy') and their parents are well-to-do.

If you don't feel comfortable with that, it's best to take six months' rent in advance or not rent to foreigners (although I think excluding anyone because of where they are from a bit unfair – but if they can't provide the assurances you are looking for or rent in advance, then it's fine). And with Right to Rent rules coming in, it's going to be even more complicated to rent to foreigners... so keep an eye on the legislation and make sure you get proof of their right to be in the UK!

Question 5.2.4: Should I charge a referencing/ admin fee?

I vote that a resounding YES! But again, it depends on your tenant type. I currently charge £200 admin/reservation fee. This is paid upfront to reserve the room and start the referencing process and is non-refundable. I've found that it just covers my costs, so I don't make a profit from it. I have to pay my letting agent for doing the viewings, pay to register the deposit, pay PayPal fees, credit check fees and so on, so the money is spent quickly.

I don't charge any renewal fees as I feel that's a bit of a

rip off. Most of my tenants convert to a statutory period tenancy when their initial AST runs out. I don't have to do any additional paperwork other than ticking a box with the deposit company to tell them the tenant is now statutory periodic.

There has been an uproar about charging admin fees to tenants and a lot of people say it just isn't right. Most letting agents charge fees to both the landlord and the tenant. With Rent to Rent you are the landlord, so unless you've done a great job negotiating, the only fee you can get is from the tenant. If tenants are willing to pay it, then I don't think there is a problem. As I said above, my £200 fee covers the costs of finding the tenant and registering their deposit. I run a business not a charity.

Question 5.2.5: What do I do with the deposit?

If you take a deposit from the tenant then you must register it with an approved company. There are two different schemes you can use.

1. Insurance based – you keep the money in your bank account.

2. Custodial – you give the money to an agency and they keep it until the end of the tenancy.

There are pros and cons to each. I use an insurance-based scheme because I like to keep the money in my bank account. This makes it easier to control how much I return of the tenant's deposit and when.

As an agent (I have to register as an agent because I don't own the houses) I must keep the money in a separate client deposit account. This is an account which has been specially set up with the bank and is ring-fenced, which means it isn't included in my business assets. So if my business were to go into administration, then no one could take the money in that account to pay my outstanding debts. It's a bit of extra admin for me to make sure the money is in the account properly (a bit of extra bookkeeping), but it makes it easier at the end of the tenancy because I can send it back to the tenant quickly or I can easily withhold it if I need to pay for damage. The tenant can still dispute it, but I already have the money, so that extra bit of control is what I find nice.

With the insurance scheme, if you need to keep some of the deposit at the end, you will have to apply to the agency to keep some of the deposit, and the tenant can dispute it and drag the process out. Also, deposit agencies do make mistakes and I've heard of them sending the deposit back when the landlord needed to keep some of it. It's then impossible to get it back. I don't like someone else being in charge of my money!

SUB-TOPIC 5.3: TENANT CONTRACTS

Question 5.3.1: What contract should I use with my tenants? A licence agreement or an AST?

This is a very common question and many people have different opinions and swear by either a licence agreement or an AST (assured shorthold tenancy). There are many other types of tenancies but I would recommend steering away from them as you start getting into longer term arrangements where it's incredibly difficult to evict tenants. I've done the research and talked to a lot of experts on this topic and here is what I have learned about Licence Agreements and ASTs:

Licence Agreements: These are used improperly by a lot of landlords as landlords believe they can give the tenant less notice if they want that tenant to leave, or they use it to make the tenant believe they can be evicted with less notice. I don't think it's right to lie to the tenant or pretend to take away their rights in this way. However, there are a few occasions when a licence agreement is correct:

1. The landlord is living in the property. If you are the landlord and you are living in the property as your main residence, then your tenants are really "lodgers" and you can use a licence agreement. Because it is your main residence and it is your home, you are able to evict a tenant much more easily. So in this situation a licence agreement is suitable.

2. The house is NOT the tenant's main residence. This is typical in more of a B&B/hotel type situation. If you have contractors living in your HMOs, these are tenants who are only staying temporarily in your area and have a permanent home they will go back to. Many of them will stay Monday to Friday or will come for three months and then finish the job they are working on and go back to their permanent home. In this situation is it also ok to use a licence agreement.

Assured Shorthold Tenancy Agreements (AST): These are to be used in most cases. In fact, if you use a licence agreement incorrectly it will automatically be treated as an AST in the eyes of the court. So in most cases it's probably best to be honest with your tenants and yourself and use an AST agreement. This is for tenants who are in your property as their main residence and when you are not living in the property yourself.

The reason landlords don't like using an AST is that it gives the tenants a lot more rights than a licence agreement does. For instance, with an AST the landlord must provide the tenant with two months' notice to evict them and can only evict them after an initial six month term. So, even if your AST with the tenant is for two months, legally you cannot evict the tenant (if they stay on) until they have been there for six months. There are also other differences between the agreements, but the main one relates to the eviction notice you can give the tenant.

It's up to you which contract you use with your tenants. We use the one from the RLA (Residential Landlords Association) which is specifically for HMOs that are rented on a room-by-room basis. We are members of the RLA and are able to use all their forms for free and are confident knowing that we always have the most up-to-date information.

Question 5.3.2: Who signs the tenancy agreement, the Rent to Renter or the property owner?

This is a bit of a grey area which happens with Rent to Rent because it is relatively new. The answer depends on what type of contract you have with the property owner (See Sub-topic 1.2: The Paperwork).

If you have a management agreement with the property owner, then you should include the property owner's name in your AST with the tenant. Depending on how your agreement is structured (and hopefully you've gone to a solicitor for the first one at least to get it done properly), you should be able to sign the agreement yourself on behalf of the owner. This is how many letting agents work. In order to be able to issue a Section 21, if you need to evict a tenant, your AST with the tenant must be set up and signed correctly and the Section 21 needs to be issued correctly based on that AST. In this situation, when issuing the Section 21 you should again have both the owner and yourself on the form.

If you have a lease agreement with the owner, then technically you are the landlord to the tenants and you will be the one who signs the AST and you don't need to have the owner's name on the AST. But this is where the grey area appears, and it hasn't been tested in the legal system relating to Rent to Rent. Ultimately, if you end up going to court with the tenant (and let's hope you've followed the tips in this book so that won't happen), it is up to the judge to decide if everything has been filled in properly. The judge is highly unlikely to have any knowledge of Rent to Rent but he will have a basic knowledge of how letting agents work. So he could just view you like any other letting agent and expect the property owner's name to be on the AST, and if it is not he can throw out your case and make you start again. This is a worst case scenario and really comes down to a technicality. What I do to get around this is I include the property owner's name on my ASTs with the tenant (as I do with those properties which are under a management agreement) but I sign it myself as the managing agent. Again, nothing has been tried and tested in the court system, but I figure it's better to be safe than sorry and adding that little bit of extra information doesn't hurt.

Question 5.3.3: Should I include a fair-use policy?

If you are paying the bills and providing the tenants with an all-inclusive rent, then I would say you should definitely have a fair-use policy in your contract with the tenants. Utility bills (especially gas and electricity) are some of the biggest variables in running an HMO and could cause significant fluctuations in your profit if you aren't able to monitor usage and pass excess charges to the tenants. Not only does having a fair-use policy protect your profits, it protects the environment as well as it keeps the tenant conscious of their energy usage and minimising it. Many tenants, when told their bills are included, stop worrying about turning off lights and electric when they leave a room, and will leave the heater running all day because they think it doesn't matter. To limit this we have a simple statement added as an 'addendum' (on an extra page that the tenant signs separately from the AST) that states our fair-use policy. I suggest you tailor this to your own circumstances and bill estimates:

> **Fair usage:** We operate a fair-use policy in respect of utilities. The fair/included amount is £400 per month for a property with up to five letting rooms. For properties with six to seven letting rooms, the fair/included amount is £450 per month.
>
> The bills and utilities included are: Gas, Electric, Water, TV Licence, Council Tax, Broadband (unlimited package) and Phone Line (for the broadband only, barred for calls). Utility usage above

the fair/included amount will be charged for on an equal split/per room basis.

We haven't had any of our houses go over this usage, although we have one which comes close due to their use of electric heaters in the winter. I've been able to remind the tenants of this clause and that they will be charged if their usage goes over. It was simply a case of telling them to turn up the temperature on their gas central heating system rather than use inefficient electric heaters in their rooms.

SECTION 6:
EVERYTHING ELSE

SUB-TOPIC 6.1: SYSTEMS

Question 6.1.1: How can I make it all easier?

Systems are the key to running a great business of any type and will greatly help in your property business. This isn't a systems manual so I won't go into too much detail, but throughout the book I have been describing a few of the systems that I use to keep things running smoothly. Let's just run through the process, from looking for a Rent to Rent property to getting it tenanted from start to finish, to help you think through the systems you need. My systems are in brackets.

First you need to advertise.

- How will you answer the calls that come in? (AllDayPA)

- How will you track what stage in the process the leads are in? (Spreadsheet or CRM system)

- How will you track your follow-ups? (Spreadsheet or CRM system)

- How will you track what form of advertising is getting you the most results? (Spreadsheet or CRM system, different phone numbers for each different advert)

- How do you deliver leaflets and ensure they are really being delivered? (Leafleting company)

- How do you mail out your HMO letters? (Virtual Assistant)

- How do you track who you meet at networking meetings and track business cards? (Mobile app CamCard)

Once you've got some property owners/agents calling you and you are out doing viewings, you need to track at what stage of the process you are with each. We initially used a spreadsheet and as we got bigger we moved to a CRM system.

Once you've signed the contract you need a process to take over the house and get it up and running. I recommend the following:

- A checklist for tracking bill and utility sign-up to make sure you've got them all and know all the account numbers.

- A checklist of all the furniture and fittings that should be in an HMO.

- A checklist of all the items that should be included on your tenant notice board and guide for the tenants living in the house.

- A checklist of key maintenance items to check through before getting tenants in.

- A list of the key dates (HMO renewal, gas safety, electric test, PAT test, etc.).

Then, when the house is all set up and ready for tenants, you need to find the tenants:

- How will you advertise? (Spareroom and own website)

- How will you track tenant enquiries? (Spreadsheet or CRM system)

- How will you track which rooms are full and when they will be empty? (Spreadsheet or CRM system)

- How will you track where tenants are with the referencing? (Spreadsheet or CRM system)

- How will you track what you need from the tenants for referencing? (Spreadsheet or CRM system)

- How will you track when tenants move in and out? (Spreadsheet or CRM system)

Whew that's a lot. And that only scratches the surface of the overall running of a property business. I recommend you start with the end in mind. If you only want one or two properties, then you can just use a quick spreadsheet. But if you want to grow and want 10, 20, 30 properties, then you should start with a good CRM system right from the beginning.

If you'd like to get started quickly, check out JADESuccess. co.uk for copies of the spreadsheets that I used in the beginning to keep track of everything, along with a lot of the other documents that I use on a regular basis to keep everything running smoothly!

Also, keep an eye on JADESimplicity.co.uk as I am working on rolling out my CRM systems package which wraps all of these areas and lists together and also links with other key programs that I use (such as Google Calendar and Mail Chimp). By using my CRM system I am able to eliminate duplicate entries of information across different platforms. I can enter a tenant or a property owner into the system when I first speak to them and then take them all the way through each stage in the system without having to update multiple spreadsheets. My partner Anthony is great with systems and has worked with a great team to get all this up and running so that everyone can benefit from it. Not only does it have the property management side (which many systems offer), but it also has the sales generation and lead follow-up as well, which most of the property management systems lack.

Finally, check the Resources section for a list of my favourite suppliers who are tried and trusted to help keep things simple for us!

SUB-TOPIC 6.2: TRAINING

Question 6.2.1: This book has been great. What's my next step if I want to learn more?

I am a strong advocate of education, whether that's a training course, a mentoring program, working with a coach or even free resources online. Let's run briefly through these options.

Free Online Resources:

Yes, that's right, I said free resources online are ok. You can find much of what you need online and there are many great forums and groups you can access without paying a penny. This is probably the slowest method, so if you have lots of time and aren't in a hurry to get started, then this could be a great method for you. Get Googling! I highly recommend my FREE Rent to Rent in the UK Facebook Group: https://www.facebook.com/groups/RenttoRentUK/

Training Courses:

There are a lot of people offering training courses. Property education is big business right now. The hardest thing is sometimes deciding which training course to do – and then being able to stop taking training courses! Most people offer free or low priced information sessions. I recommend going along to a taster session to make sure you can work well with the trainer (they all have their own personalities and you will resonate better with some). Keep in mind that most of these taster type sessions are designed to sell to you and get you to the next/higher level courses – so be prepared for some upsell.

You can get massive value from attending a one day property course, especially if you are just starting out. Try and pick one in your chosen strategy or one that covers all the strategies in an overview. It's a good way to get a basic understanding, to see if you have rapport with the trainer and know what to expect if you want to do more in-depth training. You won't be an expert in one day but you will get a lot of valuable information, not least of which will be the contacts from the networking that you will do during the coffee and lunch breaks.

After the one day course there will generally be an option/upsell to a longer course. Again, it's because you can't become an expert in one day. The next step is a weekend residential course where you can immerse yourself in the strategy with an expert. But remember to use that one day course as an interview of the trainer to make sure you would like to continue working with them.

Mentoring vs. Coaching:

There are a lot of people offering mentoring or coaching services. What is the difference and which should you choose? Although many people use these terms interchangeably, mentoring and coaching are two very different things.

Mentoring is more focused on telling you what to do – it is more directive than coaching. The person doing the mentoring needs to be an expert in the topic they are leading, as they are there to tell the mentee exactly what to do and guide them through the process. This is generally a long-term process and the mentor is there to provide support and discuss whatever the mentee is working on or struggling with.

Coaching is a step removed and coaches are there to provide more of a sounding board. The coach doesn't need to be an expert in the field. Coaches should be trained, as it is a skill to be able to question and help their coachee to think deeper about what they are doing in order to come up with their own solutions. Coaching is very task oriented, with the coachee going away from each session with tasks to achieve set goals.

I offer both coaching and mentoring with a select number of clients. I'm a trained coach with multiple certifications including ILM 5 certification and Master Coach. I'm also a Master NLP Practitioner, which means I've done a lot of training and practice on how to help people remove limiting beliefs, discover their values and reach their goals.

I'm very selective with my mentoring clients as I'm looking for people who are doers and action takers. If I'm going to spend my time with you, I want to make sure I'm spending my time with someone who is going to use the knowledge and try their hardest. There is an investment for my mentoring, but this isn't to make me rich (I make a lot more from doing deals than doing coaching and mentoring), it is to make sure my clients are really serious about investing in themselves. I'm looking for people who are serious, who don't procrastinate and who really want to achieve fantastic results!

Check out www.JADESuccess.co.uk for more information. You can get 20% off for buying our book by using the code "BOOK" when you set up your first session.

Question 6.2.2: Which course should I take?

It really depends on what you are looking for. Look at the reviews and speak to people who have done the courses to understand what they got out of them. If your particular strategy is Rent to Rent, then you can see events I'll be speaking at and our specialist rent to rent courses on offer on our website (www.JADESuccess.co.uk).

One of the biggest benefits with investing in education is the environment and support that becomes available. During the process you will meet fantastic, like-minded people who will be taking a similar journey and provide for you a lot of help and inspiration. It is highly recommended to go to some networking events offered by the training providers who you are thinking of working with to see what the general vibe is and whether you feel the environment would be supportive and positive.

SUB-TOPIC 6.3: RESOURCES

Here is a list of some of the key resources we use. They are in alphabetical order. For updates to this list please check our website – www.JADESuccess.co.uk.

Assured Shorthold Tenancy Agreement (AST): I get mine from the National Landlords Association (www.landlords.org.uk) or Residential Landlords Association (www.RLA.org.uk). By joining either of these groups you will get access to a wealth of knowledge and a great helpline anytime you have questions about tenants and tenancies. They also have contract templates for ASTs and other templates to use with your tenants.

Call Answering: AllDayPA www.alldaypa.com

Camera for taking great pictures of your rooms: Theta 360 by Ricoh. You can get it from Amazon.co.uk

Checklists: For all our checklists go to the Resources section at www.JADESuccess.co.uk

Coaching: Choose one of our coaching packages at www. JADESuccess.co.uk (20% off when you buy this book by using the code "BOOK" when you sign up).

CRM Systems

- Keep an eye on www.JADESimplicity.co.uk for the launch of our comprehensive lead tracking and property management CRM.

- Or if you want to keep it even more basic, check the Resources section on our website www.JADESuccess. co.uk for the spreadsheets we use.

Deal Calculator: Use ours at www.JADESuccess.co.uk in the Resources section.

Decorations and Fittings for an HMO

- B&M Bargains – find a store near you: www.bmstores. co.uk

- ASDA home: www.direct.asda.com

- Wilkinsons: www.wilko.com

Deposits

- MyDeposits: www.mydeposits.co.uk

- Deposit Protection: www.depositprotection.com

- Tenancy Deposit Scheme: www.tds.gb.com

Furniture: Let Us Furnish has both purchase and rental furniture and they deliver nationally: www.letusfurnish. co.uk

GoCardless: Really simple Direct Debit processing. I use this for rent collection as it keeps you informed as soon as a tenant cancels their payment or if their payment fails. We've got a free guide on "How to Easily Collect Rent" using GoCardless on our website (www. JADESuccess.co.uk). GoCardless is free to register and have a look around. Use this link to get a £50 credit from them: https://gocardless.com/?r=MVFRXVJS&utm_source=website&utm_medium=copy_paste&utm_campaign=referral_scheme_50

Hiring Remote Help: For contract workers, virtual assistants and freelancers I use www.elance.com

HMO Standards Manuals

- Gov.UK: www.gov.uk/government/.../HMO_Lic_landlords_guide.pdf)

- LACORS: www.rla.org.uk/docs/ LACORSFSguideApril62009.PDF

- National Amenity Standards for Licensed HMOs: www.rla.org.uk/landlord/guides/housing_act/ docs/all/minimum_national_amenity_standards_ for_licensable_hmos.shtml

Leaflet/Postcard printing

- Design and printing: Smart Property Leaflets: www.smartpropertyleaflets.co.uk/

- Printing: BeanPrint

- Printing: VistaPrint

- Delivery: www.dor2dor.com (This is a franchise business across the UK and has worked well for us in Oxford.)

Management Contract/Lease Agreement to use with the property owner – I recommend you have a solicitor draft your agreements in order to make sure that they are watertight. I do have some sample contracts on the JADE Success website that you can have a look at to help you understand the process and give you an idea of what should be in your contract.

Mentoring: Choose one of our mentoring packages at www.JADESuccess.co.uk (20% off when you buy this book using the code "BOOK" when you sign up).

Networking

- General Business Networking:

    - BNI (Business Networking International): www.BNI.eu

    - 4Networking: www.4networking.boz

    - Athena: www.Athenanetwork.co.uk

    - British Chamber of Commerce: www.britishchambers.org.uk

    - Business Scene: www.business-scene.com

    - Yes Group: www.yesgroup.org

- Property Networking:

    - Property Investors Network (PIN) has meetings

around the country. There are currently over 50 meetings so you should be able to find one that is local to you. These are great friendly places and always welcoming to newcomers. You can find a list of all meetings at www.PinMeeting.co.uk and you can use the voucher code "JacquieEdwards" to attend your first meeting for free!

- Berkshire Property Meet: This is one of the largest meets in the country and people flock to it on a monthly basis. http://www.berkshirepropertymeet.com/

- There are many other local networking meetings – a quick Google search should highlight some more in your area.

Online Forums

- Rent to Rent Facebook Group (Official): www.Facebook.com/groups/RenttoRentUK

- PIN Academy: www.pinacademy.co.uk

- Property Tribes: www.propertytribes.com (They also have a starter lease agreement to use with Rent to Rents.)

- HMO Facebook Group (Official): www.facebook.com/groups/housesofmultipleoccupancy/

Take some of the comments in this group and other Facebook groups with a pinch of salt. There are many people commenting on there who have very stong opinions. Remember everyone is different and different methods work in different areas. Don't get caught up in too many heated discussions!

<u>Planning Information</u>: www.planningportal.gov.uk

<u>Referencing</u>

- Letting Ref: www.lettingref.co.uk

- National Landlords Association:
  www.nlatenantcheck.org.uk

<u>Tenant Finding</u>

- www.spareroom.co.uk

- www.Gumtree.com

- www.easyroommate.com

- www.upad.com

<u>Tracking Business Cards and Contacts</u>: Phone app CamCard allows you to take pictures of the business cards you collect and it uploads the information into your mobile: https://www.camcard.com/

<u>Training Courses</u>: Sign up for our next course at www. JADESuccess.co.uk

Website Creation: In the present day and age it is important to have an online presence. I have a great team that is able to quickly put together property specific websites. We have a number of Rent to Rent template websites aimed at landlords and agents (providing you with instant credibility). The team can also help you set up a bespoke property website that you can easily maintain (no coding necessary). See www.JADEConnect.co.uk to learn more.

AUTHOR'S BIO

Jacquie Edwards started out just like everyone else working a 9-5 job in someone else's office. She knew there must be something better to life but didn't know what to do about it. She realised that she was trading her time for money and that this would only get her so far, and she needed to find financial freedom in order to live the life she deserved.

In 2013 Jacquie began her property journey with the help of some amazing friends and mentors on Simon Zutshi's Property Mastermind Courses. She and her partner were chosen as Top Performers for their target smashing results which created over £100,000 of recurring income in 12 months from property they don't even own using the Rent to Rent strategy. Now Jacquie no longer needs to work in someone else's office and is able to spend her time helping others to become Financially Free!

If you would like to accelerate your investing and work with Jacquie, please check out her website at www.JADESuccess.co.uk to schedule a FREE starter call. Times are limited so act quickly!

Printed in Great Britain
by Amazon